Liars, Thieves and
on the Bench

by Jo Carson

"Human experience is varied and astonishing, almost beyond belief, and you don't have to be on Shackleton's crew of the Endurance *to find it. It is there in your neighbors' stories."*

—Jo Carson

J o Carson is an uniquely American writer and performer, who has spent more than fifteen years working with stories from communities across the country, crafting more than thirty plays from these oral history collections. In performance, these works have illuminated and invigorated the communities in which they were forged, as the people see themselves on stage in a new light. This book collects Carson's favorite excerpts from the community plays she has written—stories that range from the homespun to the extraordinary—together creating a portrait of America in an amazing diversity and authenticity of voices. These stories are slices of life, passed beyond the circle of family and neighbors.

Jo Carson is a writer and performer living in Johnson City, Tennessee. She is the author of nine books, including short stories, books for children, and plays. *Stories I Ain't Told Nobody Yet* made Booklist's Editor's Choice and ALA's recommended list. She has received numerous national awards and grants for her plays, including an NEA Fellowship for *The Bear Facts*, the Kesselring Prize for *Day Trips* and an AT&T: OnStage Award for *Whispering to Horses*. She was a commentator on NPR's *All Things Considered*. She was an organizer of the founding meeting of Alternate ROOTS. She lives with a dog in something close to a hobbit house, newly renovated toward being green, and aspires to an edible yard in the not too distant future.

Liars, Thieves
and Other Sinners
on the Bench

Liars, Thieves
and Other Sinners
on the Bench

Jo Carson

THEATRE COMMUNICATIONS GROUP
NEW YORK
2009

This publication is made possible in part with public funds from the New York State Council on the Arts, a State Agency.

TCG books are exclusively distributed to the book trade by Consortium Book Sales and Distribution.

LIBRARY OF CONGRESS CATALOGING-IN-PUBLICATION DATA
Carson, Jo, 1946–
Liars, thieves and other sinners on the bench / By Jo Carson.—1st ed.
    p. cm.
ISBN 978-1-55936-331-0
I. Title.
PS3553.A7674L53   2009
813'.54—dc22   2009014781

Cover, book design and composition by Lisa Govan
Cover photo by Darwin Wiggett/Getty Images

First Edition, May 2009

Mixed Sources
Product group from well-managed
forests and other controlled sources
www.fsc.org Cert no. SW-COC-002283
© 1996 Forest Stewardship Council
FSC

Acknowledgments

Thanks are many on this book.

First, thanks to the people who contributed stories to the community endeavors that became the plays we made; then to the communities themselves and the people who gave time and energy to making the projects work. To list them individually would almost be to write another book, but without them, this book wouldn't be here. So, thank you all very much.

Personal thanks go to Kathy Sova, my editor at TCG, who is most gracious with my eccentricities. They are numerous, and they range from spelling to escapades with the comma queen and beyond. Years of trying to write like people talk have made for some language constructions *The Chicago Manual of Style* hasn't even dreamt of yet. I suppose I'm proud to be such a frontrunner, but I'm an editor's nightmare.

Thanks also to Al Bentz who has been my first reader for some years now. The question to him is almost always, "Does this sound right yet?" It is an odd question to put to a reader, but he gets it, and such a reader—for such a writer as this one—is a grace.

Contents

Contents

Contents

Contents

About the Making
of the Work

Fact and Fiction

I once sat across lunch from an elderly lady who had, up until the previous month, been the county historian of ———— County, Tennessee.

County historian is a position of some honor and no pay in the rural South. You earn it by a life-long passion for local history and longevity. The payoff is that when the local newspaper needs to check a local historical fact, they call the county historian, who tells them, to the best of his/her knowledge what that information is, and then that fact appears in the paper prefaced by So and So, county historian.

Honor, but no pay.

But this lady was no longer the official county historian, because she had had a falling out with the rest of the historical society, and been officially removed from the job. I'm not sure how you officially remove a county historian, most of them are buried before they are removed. And this was an odd removal, because the newspaper still called this woman since she knew more than anybody else, even though historical facts were now prefaced by So and So, ———— County's unofficial historian.

So, she'd lost the position but not the function.

I was at lunch with her because, what was unspoken but implied to me, was that the project I was working on would go much easier if she liked me. I was doing my damnedest to be charming. Charm is not the strongest act in my repertory, I have to work at charm and, even then, I'm better from a distance. Lunch is close quarters.

I am a scribbler, and the truth is I am best left alone in my habitat with the tools of my trade, and allowed out only occasionally in the sort of endeavor (a performance situation) that keeps a comfortable distance between me and an audience.

I was not in my habitat at this lunch. I was out trying to earn a living in a restaurant that suffered from an excess of hanging plants and chicken dishes. The project was paying for the feeding; the ex-county historian ordered a tremendous amount to eat, including two desserts. I ordered a garden salad and iced tea.

We make small talk: "I'm from Upper East Tennessee, Johnson City," I tell her.

"Republicans," she snarls.

And it is true. One election I remember, the democrat I voted for got three votes, one was mine, one was his, and I'd give eyeteeth to know who the other was. Probably his mother.

I tell her this story, she is not amused. She is not amused with any of my stories.

I even try the one about being middle-aged and taking up with my first horse. I say it was my mid-life crisis, I say I took up with a horse instead of a new man or a Mazeratti; everybody else in the world laughs at that line, smiles at the very least, but not the ex-county historian.

"Gone to horses," she says.

It's a lot like gone to the devil. Gone to frivolous things. People are never "gone to cows." Cows are a living. We eat them, but not in this restaurant.

"Well," she finally says, "what is it you want from me?"

And I explain that I am a playwright and that I have been hired to make a performance piece, a play, out of the oral histories that are being collected in that county.

This is hard because we are both hard of hearing and the restaurant is very noisy.

"But what do you want from me?" she yells. We are attracting the attention of the other diners because we are talking so loud.

Your blessing, your help, access to your knowledge . . . I think. What do I have to ask for? What should I ask for to get me in good with her? I don't know. So I say, "Your story, too."

"My story, is it? I despise you and your kind."

This woman is no better at charm than I am.

"Artists, all of you! You have no respect for facts!"

All right. There were five people who voted for the democrat, and I couldn't afford a Mazeratti if I wanted one. I said, "I beg your pardon?"

"Artists have no respect for facts. I am a historian. I love facts. If you find you want facts, you can ask for them and I will give them to you, but you won't be interested in facts, artists never are. You want 'my story.' Well, I don't tell stories, and I don't much care for people who do. I really don't think we have anything more to say to one another."

And she ordered to-go boxes for her remaining lunch and two desserts—I guess she wanted to have her carrot cake and eat her coconut—and I took her and her meal remains back home. I had to help her carry her lunch into her house.

I can see how she and the rest of the historical society might have had a falling out.

But she is right, you know, at least about me. I'm guilty as charged. Facts are not what I'm most interested in, I like stories better, always have. And my Grandma Carson admonished her daughter, a woman who couldn't tell a story to save her soul, not to ruin a good story by sticking to facts—*she* never did—and I was a child at that dinner table.

I took that advice to heart, I have never been overly constrained by facts myself, especially in the telling of good stories, an inclination that got me in a lot of trouble as a child, but has served me very well, later, as a writer.

So, in honor of the ex-county historian, I want to shore up this untrustworthy art with a few assorted facts.

First: the pieces you will read come from real people and real oral histories, but oral histories are people's memories, and memory is a notoriously bad historian. What is caught in memory is another kind of truth besides the facts, often just as valid.

Second: a few of the pieces began with two or three lines in an oral history about something else besides the story, and the digression was compelling enough that I made something of it that surprised everybody.

Or often, I have condensed twenty or thirty pages of rambles into two or three minutes of cogent story.

Or I have combined different people's stories to make a more interesting piece for the stage.

Or, most likely, some combination of all of the above.

In oral histories, people don't talk the way these scripts go; these are, at the very least, crafted stories.

What is true, the bottom-line fact of this work, is that it is rooted in real experience and a series of specific places, which is the stuff of art and history both, and it is very hard to separate them.

This is one of three stories in this book that is not a piece I wrote from oral histories for one play or another. The other two pieces are Thousands *from the* Women and Mice *section and* White Coyote, *a follow-up to the* Covet *story in the* Troubles and Fears *section. This* Fact and Fiction *story and the* Thousands *story are mine. The events happened to me, I narrate them. The* White Coyote *story was told to me. I never used it in a play, but after it happened—some months after we'd done the play that used the* Covet *story— I came to think the* Covet *story should not be told again without its follow-up, so* White Coyote *is included here.*

I do use the stories in this book: I tell them in a one-woman show. This story about lunch with the ex-county historian is often my introduction to what follows in a performance, which is why it also leads this book. What I do in performance is a reading by a writer, in the tradition of Mark Twain when he rented a hall and began doing lectures. (Credit where credit is due: I might not even know of Mark Twain's lectures without Hal Holbrook's work.) I name Mark Twain as much in evocation as anything else, but if I have a teacher—a mentor of what the hard riotous irony of this world is and isn't—I have just named him.

The Process

The process of this oral history/community work has evolved as follows: I sometimes teach people how to collect stories; sometimes I'm taught by someone who really knows his or her community, but communities collect their own stories. This is no small or easy endeavor, first because good stories are hard to come by, and, second, because I need a lot of them (or a few very good ones) to write a collaborative piece.

It is important that each community collect its own stories. People are more open to talk with people they know or have something in common with than with writer-type strangers. So I get better stories if the community participates in the collecting of them.

More important, gathering stories is an investment of time and energy in the project by people who want to see it happen. Excellent stuff—that kind of investment, the stuff of intent. These projects do not happen anywhere but on the surface without that sort of local investment. And I'm spoiled—surface scratching isn't good enough anymore.

There is a progression here that should be mentioned: once a community finds me or a given team relatively trustworthy in our use of their stories, a whole different level of story starts to come. So stories get richer as work in a place progresses. A community does not ever run out of stories, they just get deeper and richer.

Next, the collected oral histories are transcribed and then sent to me. I read carefully, I visit a place, time and again—I spend time, talk with people (anybody and everybody), follow up on stories when I'd like more information about something, and write a piece from the stories for public performance in and by that community.

My job is to deal honestly with a community, and sometimes that means I push people. I don't back off from hard stories; a community is never ever served by something that is just cute and trite. The pieces I write are not traditional plays either, they are often (some of) the stories of a place put together like quilts around themes, or with some individual's story as a backbone for a piece.

Most of the time, it is nonprofessional people who are performing in the shows with the aid of a director who is as interested in community as I am. (Richard Geer, one of my directors, has done considerable thinking and writing on the subject. You can find a lot about him and his work on the www. Jerry Stropnicky has also written some on the subject.) For these projects, everyone who wants to participate is included in some way. The process of art is (or should be) as important as the product generated. The piece is rehearsed in, and by, and performed for, the community it comes from. So these projects are actually a very old kind of theater in which the tellers and the stories and the audience are not separate from one another at all, and for that they can be the most relevant and moving presentations I've seen yet on stage.

The Projects

Lima, Ohio: a one-time endeavor with a group of community people and Cornerstone Theater. The community group hired all of us. Lima has acres if not miles of environmentally problematic industrial ruin, the Lima Steam Engine was built there. When diesel engines moved into railroad use, they were built elsewhere. The community was interested in trying to do something for, with, to, about the industrial ruin, the Lima rustbelt economy, and the extraordinary history around the Lima Steam Engine (railroad history). The play was not produced beyond public readings, money was not available. But I loved the patternmaker, he's the first man in the industrial process without whom those steam engines would have stayed on paper.

Colquitt, Georgia, "Swamp Gravy": a successful economic development endeavor funded originally by some truly visionary local people. "Swamp Gravy" is close to eighteen years old and is still in operation. I wrote their first six or seven years of shows, depending on what is counted as new shows. (swampgravy.com)

Belle Glade, Florida, "Pot Luck in the Muck": an attempt at making a "Swamp Gravy" clone in another place. I wrote two shows for them. Belle Glade is an extraordinary place; it is muck land uncovered from the Everglades by the building of the dike around Lake Okeechobee. Muck land is so rich that it can catch fire just from the Florida sun shining on it. And anything that can tolerate heat will grow like gangbusters in it, it is very rich. Much of Belle Glade is owned by agribusiness now, the single industry is farming or farming-related (besides the tourists that visit Lake Okeechobee), and most of the migrant labor in the east spends the winter and starts the picking season in Belle Glade. I did not lack for stories. The project lacked for money to continue.

Walton County, Florida, "Grit and Grace": another clone of "Swamp Gravy." I wrote the first two shows for them. The project is ongoing with local talent. (gritandgrace.com)

Newport News, Virginia, "Yoder Barn": close to ten years old with five new plays (and several serious rewrites) and this project is ongoing. This was something of a "restoration of soul" project. The Mennonite community there lost farms and a way of life to strip malls and subdivisions. One family had a barn they couldn't bring themselves to destroy. They turned it into a performing space and then needed something to perform in it. The first show I did for them was an anniversary piece that celebrated a hundred years of that community in that place, and we've been working together ever since. Management of the barn has recently been turned over to a local university.

Southeastern Georgia (actually three small towns: St. Mary's, Woodbine and Kingston), "Crooked Rivers": a "Swamp Gravy" model. Their first play was in 2006. This project hopes to be ongoing.

Harlan, Kentucky, "Higher Ground": intends to be ongoing. Their second play was spring 2009. A third is planned. (www.secc.kctcs.edu; select Appalachian Center)

Lancaster, Pennslyvania, The Fulton Opera House: a one-time story play project. The Fulton is ongoing as a professional theater. (www.atthefulton.org)

East Tennessee: a one-time endeavor, a collection of women's stories from Upper East Tennessee.

Etowah, Tennessee: a one-time story play around L&N Railroad stories.

Chicago, Illinois, "Scrap Mettle Soul": ongoing, I wrote their first two shows, which were both made of stories from a new SRO, mentored a second playwright, and then mentored a third. (www.scrapmettlesoul.org)

Port Gibson, Mississippi, Mississippi Cultural Crossroads: MCC does a lot of great performance work—a *Romeo and Juliet* across race, for example, with a black Romeo and a white Juliet with Cornerstone Theater. MCC has served as producer for an impressive list of people and groups who are about community and more: Carpetbag Theater, John O'Neal, Roadside Theater, Liz Lerman and others. Nayo Watkins wrote a play from oral histories about civil rights struggles; I wrote a piece from other oral histories. They also have an ongoing young people's theater/literacy project, Peanut Butter & Jelly Theater, which creates some of their own work and tours. They have been about collecting oral histories and the good use of them for a lot of years, and they have an astonishing collection of stories. Mississippi Cultural Crossroads also includes an economic aspect: truly extraordinary quilts are made there and available for sale, and quilt making is taught by some real masters. Visit their website for the quilts if nothing else. (www.msculturalcrossroads.org)

Chota, Montana: Chota has a dryland wheat farmer turned arts entrepreneur living there: "You plow and plant and harvest that many acres, you have a lot of time driving around in fields to think about other things." This man's wife and her cousin were the playwrights for their project. They've done one play that I know of. I was hired for some one-time writing instruction. One piece in this collection from Chota, *Fire*, was the working piece I used for what little instruction I ended up doing. They didn't need me. But I had an amazing trip anyway, and I wrote *Thousands* from the Women and Mice section out of that experience.

Sautee-Nacoochee, Georgia, "Headwaters": an ongoing project. Sautee-Nacoochee is located at the beginning of the spine of the Appalachian Mountains in northeast Georgia. Rabun Gap and the ongoing Foxfire endeavor come from close by. Rich territory, good stories, and the best community team I've worked with. As I write this, we are working on the second show of at least three for the "Headwaters" project. The 2009 production was designed by Lynn Jeffries, designer and puppet master of Cornerstone Theater, so the piece from S-N in this book includes a puppet of a horse whose name is Cowboy, and a human, the horse's owner, Jim-bo.

A lot of the places I have worked are not what you ever think of as destination spots. I sometimes say of some of these projects (not all of them) that a community has to get pretty desperate to think art might fix something. I say it as a joke but it really isn't. Art is never likely to change the economy of a place; we as a culture don't value art or artists enough for the economics of art to make much impact. But art is capable of changing people's perception of a place and of themselves and of their neighbors in a way that nothing else can. I see that time and again. A change in perception can change the economy and anything else you care to name. It takes a kind of single-minded determination and so much work that some of the people behind these projects, especially the ongoing ones, should be recognized as saints. Saint Joy of Colquitt. Saint Robert of Harlan. Saint Patty of Port Gibson. There is never much glory or even enough acknowledgment for the kind of work it takes to do this stuff. So I want to make at least a nod in the right direction.

———

More of these stories are included in Spider Speculations: A Physics and Biophysics of Storytelling *by the same author.*

The Collaborators

T he first collaborators in these projects are obviously
the communities themselves. The next level of collaborators are the professionals who work with the production of the plays I write. There is some history . . .

Cornerstone Theater comes up three times in the projects
list above. Cornerstone has been about community work in this
country for more than twenty years, and the work they do is,
and has been, astonishing. The play at Lima, Ohio, was with
Cornerstone; many years later a Cornerstone intern, Maya
Gurantz, directed the play I wrote for Port Gibson, Mississippi.
And designer Lynn Jeffries is working with the "Headwaters"
project in Georgia. (www.cornerstonetheater.org)

Dr. Richard Owen Geer first, and later Geer with Jules
Corriere, who make up the directing partnership of Community Performance, Inc., have directed the majority of the community plays I have written. I also mentored Jules (as if she
needed it!) as another playwright, and she and I wrote four
shows together for a monster of a stories project in Colorado.
I have not included any of that work in this book. Jules has several shows of her own under her belt now, and she is the pri-
mary playwright for Community Performance, Inc. Commun-

ity Performance, Inc. comes to these story play projects with an artistic package that includes director, writer, designers and a choreographer (Joe Varga for stage design, Brackley Frayer for lights and Iega Jeff for movement). (www.comperf.com)

Jerry Stropnicky of the Bloomsburg Theatre Ensemble was the director for the Harlan, Kentucky, project and for Georgia's *Crooked Rivers* project. He worked with "Swamp Gravy" for several years, and he's a founding member of Bloomsburg Theatre Ensemble. He has been an actor, director, writer and any number of other necessary things with BTE for years. (www.bte.org)

Sally Rogers is the composer on the projects for the Yoder Barn. The Mennonites have a tradition of vocal music, and the shows we do for them are musicals (called folk operas by the community). Sally writes to the community strength. She has also written music for shows in other places as needed. I can call this woman on the phone, describe the situation, describe the song I need and what I need it to do, and Sally does it. (www.sallyrogers.com)

And often, in the process of a production, someone with specific skills from a community will come forward. I've had other composers and cloggers and bluegrass bands and choirs, a gospel quartet and gymnasts and jugglers, puppeteers . . . The intent is always to use what skills people bring and want to contribute, so we do that.

Instructions for This Book

The material in this book was first intended for performance, so have fun, practice your acting, and read it aloud at least once.

The material in this book is a series of separate stories. They do not follow one another here except by theme. They were not quite such stand-alone pieces when they were parts of plays, but they are stand-alone pieces in this book. So feel free to read them, digest them, consider them, a few at a time.

Many of the single stories in this book used differently could have been a novel or a full-length play. Instead, the stories came to me to make a very specific kind of story play about a series of specific communities. So they got used as a sort of verbal photograph; this book is sometimes almost a photograph album. Odd use for such stories as some of these are but, without such use, how would we know them?

Read the stories for the extraordinary experience they hold. The human condition is almost beyond imagining, and you will get a sense of that here.

People tend to go story collecting in a different generation than their own, mostly an older generation, and this book reflects that inclination. Read it as a kind of history: it is.

Close History

A Civil War Story

East Tennessee

WOMAN: It was about as hard a time as the Lord ever made, that war, and we were living hand to mouth to start with. We had forty acres, but it was more rocks than dirt. We had a milk cow, and hogs and chickens—well, we had that at the beginning of the war, but towards the end anybody coming through took and ate whatever you had. Especially the Confederates, those men were hungry. So, after a while, what we had left was a milk cow and a horse, and we had that because our farm had a cave on it, and anytime we heard about soldiers being in our area, my husband would take the animals back into that cave. There was a creek ran out of it, and he'd walk those two up the creek, bring them out again at night to graze, and spend daylight back in the cave. The Confederates wanted him as badly as they wanted the animals, they were running out of men to fight, so it was all three of them that were hiding. My husband did not want to fight because he did not want to have to fight against the South, but he did not believe in what the South was doing. So he hid, too. Except it was hard to hide from neighbors. And to make a long story short, there was a band of Confederates that learned he was hiding out, and instead of giving them all away, my husband allowed himself to be caught, leaving me the horse and the cow still hidden in the cave.

MAN (*A letter*): My darling daughter, I have been two weeks finding a pen, a scrap of paper and a sealing stamp. Know, as I write this, I am safe and not yet gone as they would have me. You should burn this when you finish reading it, because I know now who told I was still there. You will know soon enough, if you don't already, she will likely be the first to ask after me, she will come to your house, and if you are not there, she will feel free to look for letters. She is kin to me. Say to everyone you have not heard from me. It is a risk to write at all. But I do it for your heart's comfort. Not fifty miles from there, I saw an opportunity and I took it. The men did not hold me prisoner, exactly, I was not bound, but I was watched. And the afternoon of the second day, we had made a raid for food and found a cow and liquor, and I let them think I was drinking with them as if I was one of them, until we had eaten our fill, and they were drunk. I walked into the woods as if I was going in service of my bodily functions, and did not come back. I knew the mountains and they did not, and I was not impaired with anything but the night, and they were. I have thought about what to do, and I cannot come back there. I am thinking of going on into Kentuck for reasons you already know. I love you. Your mother.

WOMAN: He said "your mother" so if someone did read the letter, I could make up some story or claim I did not know what it was about. But the seal on it was not broken, so it had not been read, and I knew from it that he was going to join the Union Army. And four months later . . .

MAN (*Another letter*): My darling wife, I am in the hospital at Lexington, Kentucky, and I am no longer of any use to either army, so they are quite willing to discharge me if I can get a way home. If you still have Kate, she could do it. I shall try to wait for you. Your husband.

WOMAN: I did not know what to expect, he did not say how bad he was hurt, and I did not know how to do it, but yes, I still had Kate, my cave horse, Kate. She was used to the dark and that was good. I had to go to Lexington. We traveled at night. Kate would have made someone a fine feast, if not a fast trip home, and there were plenty who would have been willing to eat horse flesh. Would have shot the horse out from under me if they had seen her. Or taken her for themselves. A civilian with a horse was rare, the armies had them all. So I put my husband's saddle on Kate, and dressed myself in his old clothes. I looked a little like a boy. I hoped I was too young a boy to be conscripted. And then, to get into Kentucky, I had to go through the pass at Cumberland Gap. There is a cave at Cumberland Gap, and it was used sometimes as a hospital by one side or the other. At that time, it was held by Confederates, and I swear, you could smell the dying from the bottom of the mountain. Kate was terrified for the smell of so much blood, and I knew it was what we were going into in Lexington. I didn't know yet what had happened to my husband, and I couldn't keep from throwing up. We were a pretty sight, going over that mountain in the dark, Kate crazed, me puking. It was a wonder Kate didn't take us both over the side, and there were moments when I would have just as soon gone.

MAN: I am no longer of any use to either army, so they are quite willing to discharge me if I can get a way home.

WOMAN: We moved at night; even then, we moved as much off the roads as on them. I have a fair sense of direction, and I was never far from a road, but I was twenty-three days getting to Lexington. I had to beg or hunt food, and Kate, too, had to be fed. I carried a dress with me, and if I had to beg food, I would tie Kate where she could not be seen easily, change clothes, and walk to a house. I could not say I was going to Lexington to get my husband for fear I was begging from Confederate sympathizers. I said I had news of my mother's very serious illness and I was trying to see her before she died. People thought I was soft in the head. So many were lost, so many had died, that an old woman dying in her own bed seemed like a gift, and her daughter should stay home and pray for her soul and be happy for her.

MAN: I shall try to wait for you.

WOMAN: By the time I got to him, the doctors had amputated both his legs at the knees to keep him from dying of gangrene. He was alive, but barely. I was his nurse there, for a few days, a week, but I came to believe that staying in that hospital was a greater danger than leaving it. I did not know what I could do with him, he could not sit on any horse, he could not tolerate the pain, or keep his balance, or keep the blood he had left in his body, or, for that matter, keep conscious, not with new stumps for legs, so I made a litter out of poles and blankets. I looked for a cart but there was none to be had. I tied the litter to the stirrups of the saddle and tied him onto it, I led Kate, and started home. We could not travel at night or off the road. He was too close to dead. I thought surely no one will bother me with this burden, but I pulled my gun on a soldier who tried to take Kate. We were camped, and something was bothering her and so I went to look, and there was this man. I told him I would shoot him as dead as any soldier would, and he said he was just trying to go home to his wife, and I told him to walk. I said, "You can walk, and you would steal from a man who has no other way home?" He told me he could still get home and it didn't look to him like we were going to make it. I said, "Curse you. Leave my horse, or I will kill you." It is the only time in my life yet I have felt or said such as that. We were thirty days coming home, this time begging food and shelter much more often, and for a day or two at a time until he had the strength to move again. I needed clean water and bandages, we had to beg them, too. He wore his clothes, I wore my own this time. We passed, again, the cave at Cumberland Gap. We passed it during the day this time, we had to. I uncovered the stumps of his legs, him, barely conscious on the litter, I left them open to be seen by everyone who cared to look, and I led Kate through. You would have thought we were a parade for the men who lined the road to look at us, most of them missing something. No words were spoken. Kate was frightened again for the smell, and not easy to handle. A Confederate officer stepped forward, one of his arms was gone, and he asked if I needed help, and I told him it was the smell of so much blood and death that spooked the horse, that we would be fine once we were past. And he said, "Yes, spooks me, too." And he took the other side of Kate's halter with the arm he had left, and walked with us till Kate calmed down. "Nice horse," he said, "good thing you still got her." And that was all he said of Kate.

My husband began to gain strength again once we got home.

MAN: I need two oak posts, and carving tools.

WOMAN: And he made himself pegs for his lower legs, and learned to walk on them.

MAN: I always did want to be a taller man.

WOMAN: He got to where he could ride again. I plowed and planted that spring, but he did it the next year. It cost him in pain but he did it.

MAN: I'm going to see if I can find a stallion I like, and breed Kate to him.

WOMAN: He came home instead with a big jackass.

MAN: He's going to make our living. You watch.

WOMAN: Kate produced a fine mule, and then another one, and we sold those two for a team and bought mares, and my husband turned himself into a mule breeder. After a while, he hired our fields plowed and planted and our hay cut. It was timely, and he was right, that jackass did make our living. Right after the war, everybody needed mules again, everybody. And we raised good ones and sold them for fair prices.

The Union hospital at Lexington is fact. The hospital at Cudjo's Cave at Cumberland Gap is a strong local story. The story is that the cave was used by the wounded from both sides, Union and Confederate, at different times during the war. There is no question that both the Union and Confederate troops were through Cumberland Gap, and a cave would be shelter, so I used it, too. This woman—it was her elderly granddaughter who told the story— did have to go through Cumberland Gap to get to Lexington.

Great-Grandfather

Chicago, Illinois

AN OLDER MAN: I met my great-grandfather once—I was seven.

He had served in the Civil War—he had a mini ball in his hip, and he died of that. Lead poisoning. I mean, he willed himself dead, I think. He didn't want to die of old age, and he was already ninety-three when I met him, and—the story goes—he seemed fine one afternoon when he laid down on his bed to rest but he didn't get up, and the next day he was dead.

They did an autopsy because there hadn't been anything discernable wrong with him. The only thing they could find was the lead. But he'd carried that mini ball around more than three-quarters of his life and it didn't kill him till he was ready to die. Willful man.

I met him that once, and at seven, I had the audacity to ask if there was anything special he had to say to me. And he said there was, that when he was my age, the men who sat on the square in town had wounds from the Revolutionary War. That he remembered one man in particular who had a hunchback he got for a grapeshot wound at Bunker Hill.

He took my hand. He said you touch me. I touched them. You are not so far away as you think from the making of this country.

I love that. I think of that.

I made a sculpture of a pig once, a hog, life-size, and I put it in our living room. My children wanted to know why on earth we had to live with that. My granddaddy went West, not the great-granddaddy, just granddaddy, and he and grandmother and their new baby—my father—ended up spending the winter on the plains in a sod house with their animals and three other people.

The animals were inside for their warmth, there was no wood for a fire. They cooked on a dung fire.

They started that winter with a pair of pigs, but they ate the pigs because they were desperate, and eating the pigs seemed like a better idea than eating the milk cow. I told my children it was not so long ago their people lived very close with the real thing, and, here, in a nice house in an amazing city—somebody told me there are 120 languages spoken at the high school four blocks from my house—I made the pig because I wanted to keep myself in mind of how close we are to our past.

I touched a man who had touched a man who fought in the Revolutionary War.

Places

Sometimes, I do a piece for a show about a specific place, but "place" can be different things. The first story here is about a building; the second—The Fulton—is a genuine piece of American theatrical history; the third is literally geology; the fourth is a kind of history.

The Yoder Barn

Newport News, Virginia

A Narrator and the Owner.

NARRATOR: This is a theater with a story. It started as a barn,
and it is a barn with a story. If you know carpentry, you can
likely read it yourself, but for those who don't, some history.

Barns are usually what's called vernacular construction.

They were laid out and built by the folks who used them
and they were built of local material. Really local material.
Trees that were cut from the farm where the barn was built.
This is especially true of old barns.

But this one is a balloon-frame, bow-truss barn. It is a
fairly recent idea as barns go. Comes out of the fire that
burnt Chicago.

Older barns were post-and-beam construction.

You set up posts, you laid beams across the top, and this
was the support for the roof. The first floor of this barn is
a post-and-beam construction, and this floor is laid on the
beams and the foundation. The posts and beams in old
barns were usually oak or some other seasoned hardwood.
The logs were often hewn by hand and they could be as big
as a foot square and as long as the tree was tall in a single

trunk, provided you could move it to where you wanted the barn. Or if you were willing to build your barn where you dropped the trees.

But the problem with the posts and beams was the posts. They get in the way. You can drive a tractor and wagon into this barn, unload your hay, turn it around and drive out again.

But not so down on the ground floor of this barn because of the posts.

Now when Chicago burnt, they needed to find an economical way to rebuild everything. George Washington Snow had come up with using light, rigid, timber frames about forty years before, but that idea hadn't been used much at all until after that fire.

The light timber construction was dubbed a balloon frame because, at first, people were sure it would blow away in a strong wind.

And the basic idea of a balloon frame is a lot of smaller supports on the outside walls. No huge internal posts and beams.

OWNER: The first balloon-frame barn my father saw was in Ohio. We were there visiting relatives, and on an adjoining farm was this fancy new barn and we made a special excursion to see it. This was a revolution of a barn, and the whole community was proud of it. My father looked at the inside of it, all that space with no posts, and said if his ever burnt, he'd build the new one like this. In a few days, we came back home: it was dark as we got there, and there was the glow of a fire on the horizon. Our barn was on fire. The old barn was gone by the time we got there except for the foot-square posts. They were curled like matchsticks. We had run a dairy out of that barn, and the next milking was at midnight and the cows don't wait because the barn burnt down. So we had to make do for the milking. My father eventually built the first modern milking parlor around here, but at first, we just made do. He began cutting timber for the new barn the next day and he wrote back up to

Ohio, wanted to know who built that barn he liked, wanted to hire him, but the man from Ohio couldn't build a barn in Virginia because there was a patent on that barn. But there was a man in Virginia who could build one. Over in the Shenandoah Valley. An Amish man named Dan Martin, a peg-legged man whose leg squeaked like it needed oil when he walked. My father went to talk to him. A month later, Dan Martin came here with his sons for carpenters, and a daughter to cook for them. My father went and got them. Dan Martin didn't drive.

NARRATOR: Now about that patent. Folks knew a good idea when they saw one, and mail-order catalogs, Sears and Roebuck, began selling balloon-frame kits for "bunga-lows" shortly after the Chicago fire. The kit came by rail-road and contained all the precut lumber necessary to assemble the structure for a specific house plan. If you bought a fancy kit, you even got the front porch trim.

They were cheap and relatively easy to put together and they sold like crazy. All over the country. You know the Grant Woods painting, *American Gothic*, the farmer stand-ing there with his pitchfork and his wife . . . well, there is joke in that painting. The house behind them is a Sears and Roebuck kit house.

And people started trying to build balloon-frame barns. The barns were actually harder. So much bigger. So Sears and Roebuck developed and sold a kit of precut lumber for a balloon-frame, bow-truss barn, because it was the mea-suring and the cutting of the angles—the piecing together, just to name it—that was hard to get right.

OWNER: Now, my father was not opposed to using a good idea, but the kits weren't for as big a barn as he needed, and Dan Martin was not a man who put much stock in Sears and Roebuck anyway, and the lumber for the new barn was already cut from the farm. It took Dan Martin and his sons three months to put up the structure.

NARRATOR: The siding and the roofing are traditionally left for the farmer to do in all his spare time.

OWNER: That's between the crops and the noon and the mid-night milking . . . They built the floor first and laid out the pattern for the trusses and assembled them on the floor and stood them into place with winches and ropes and a trac-tor or two if I remember right. I was nine.

NARRATOR: Dan Martin was an excellent carpenter, and he intended his barns to stand a long time.

OWNER: And stand it did, and put in its first fifty years of ser-vice as a barn.

NARRATOR: Then it became a traveling barn.

OWNER: When we decided to make a theater of it, it had to be moved.

NARRATOR: You heard him. Moved. Picked up, put on wheels and towed behind bulldozers.

OWNER: A quarter of a mile from where it first stood.

NARRATOR: A white elephant if ever there was one.

OWNER: It's true, but the barn itself was actually the easy part, you should have seen us moving the silo and the handmade brick-milking parlor.

NARRATOR: The foundation and first floor are new here, but the wooden barn is Dan Martin's original.

OWNER: Just thought you might like to know where you are.

———

The Yoder Barn at Oyster Point Road and Jefferson Avenue in Newport News, Virginia, is one of the most extraordinary performance spaces I've had the privilege to work in. It is a barn, long narrow space—the man whose father had it built, the owner from the piece above, says, "Well, it would be a different shape if cows were bigger animals." Acoustics in it are so good that it often gets used as a concert hall. Mennonite tradition includes lots of choral music, and Mennonite hymns are about making a joyful (and beautiful) noise, so among the uses for the barn in that particular community are hymn-sings. These are mostly hymns I'd never even heard before I started working with these folks (I was raised Baptist—didn't take—not Anabaptist). The music used is a real celebration. I'm actually recommending a hymn-sing at the barn.

The Fulton Opera House

Lancaster, Pennsylvania

Old

An old Woman and the Stage Manager are the characters. The old Woman is a real actor's part. She is in a wheelchair; she is pushed on stage by the Stage Manager. When the lights come up on her . . .

WOMAN: Well, I wondered if they had light in here. Most everybody's got the juice now, it's uncommon not to have it, but I was beginning to wonder. Make me sit back there in the dark. But they have juice. I'm glad to know they've not fallen behind the times.

A little more juice than they need if you ask me.

(She looks around for a moment, tries to see from under the lights.)

They told me when the lights come on to start talking, but I don't see anybody to talk to. Who am I supposed to talk to? Is anybody here?

STAGE MANAGER: You're supposed to tell about the Fulton, remember?

WOMAN: No.

STAGE MANAGER: Your granddaddy started it.

WOMAN: My granddaddy was a corset maker. He started off as a servant that came to this country, and he had to work for seven years on a farm and he didn't like it, so he became a corset maker for horses, you know, corsets so you could hook them to a buggy and he liked the theater and he started one at Fulton Hall. He liked it better than the farm or the horses either.

STAGE MANAGER: Your granddaddy was a harness maker.

WOMAN: What do you think I said he was? Now, we had a horse at the beginning, we had to go around and change the signs, and the horse got to know where they were, and she'd just walk from sign board to sign board and wait for you. Sometimes I see her in the refrigerator.

STAGE MANAGER: Your granddaddy, Blasius Yecker . . .

WOMAN: I don't know exactly when he started a theater, sometime when I was a child, and I don't hardly ever remember being a child though I'm sure I was one once. Started it because some lady . . . There was three stories in the building, a shooting gallery and beer hall upstairs, and manure storage downstairs, and it was a hot summer day so the smell was coming up, and somebody shot a hole in the floor up above, and spilled beer poured through it onto her recitation, and she got mad, and said this town had no culture and she wasn't coming back till we got some, and she was famous, so Granddaddy bought the place and made a theater. And people came. Most of them sat in the seats, but sometimes they got up on stage. I met . . . oh . . . what was her name? All you had to do was put her name on a sign and people would line up to buy tickets. I met her. She was a dancer and she was very good at dying. And she didn't want to go out the stage door. Didn't want to go out back, she wanted the theater left open with all the lights on so she could walk through that way and come out the front door at night. Last time she came, she only had one leg. She could still die just fine. And she did, eventually.

And that family, most of them were men, but there was a mother, too. I guess she was the mother. Somebody had to be the mother. They liked the plays where you died at the end, too. They had big voices, all of them, and they did a lot of . . . what's that English fellow that wrote too much? Most of it was hard to understand, but it had sword fights, and people stabbing one another all in it. And the people you liked the best always had to die in the end. Well, this family were all very good at dying, too, every one of them, so they did a lot of that English fellow. They acted like they were English, I thought.

There was another family that was here, too, but one of them had shot the president. He wasn't ever here, he was dead by them, just his brothers and uncles and cousins, and maybe their dogs, too, but I don't know for sure about the dogs . . .

Did those people have the dogs?

STAGE MANAGER: Maybe we should see if we can refresh your memory . . .

WOMAN: That's not all I've got to tell, I just wanted to know if those people had dogs . . .

STAGE MANAGER: I don't know who had the dogs.

WOMAN: You are no better off than I am. There is a bullet hole somewhere in here. It's been fifty years since I was even here, and this is the first time I've ever been on the stage. I never went anywhere but the ticket offices. So I don't remember where—somewhere there—a bullet hole. What was his name? He had long wavy hair and his coat had long fringe all on the sleeves. He had Indians in the show. Real ones that said things they'd really said. About what white people did to them, but he'd taken away their bows and arrows. And a girl who could shoot the centers out of cards, she's the one left the bullet holes in the walls. It was all cowboys and horses, and they were all on stage here. They went out the back door. Came in the back door, too. Didn't have to leave the lights on for them.

And the big woman, she was from Kansas, who was she? Stood right up here. She didn't want anybody to even see anything alcoholic to drink, I expect she didn't even like the alcohol to rub on you when you're sore. Or old. She showed how to bust a keg up with an ax. Maybe she just talked about busting kegs up with her ax, but she had her own ax and she wanted all the women here to get their own axes and go out and do it. It was her speech. We had speeches, too.

My granddaddy didn't like her much, and he told me not to get any ideas.

And there was a mathemagician who made beautiful women just go away. Put them in a box and poof! Poof! Smoke and everything. One of them didn't come back. I think he was dangerous. He looked at you like he might be dangerous, you know, he had sneaky eyes and a way of waving his hands around like he knew things you didn't. He sawed one of the women up. Sometimes he came and sat in the ticket office. He said she ran away, the one that didn't come back, but I'm not so sure. Who-done-it! That was his name. I always thought we should have looked in the basement, but I didn't ever go to the basement. Things happened in the basement of that building. I stayed in the ticket office. I sold tickets. Sixty years of selling tickets.

And then there was the man who said rumors of his demise were greatly exaggerated. I liked that. He was from the Mississippi River and he talked about living out there on the Mississippi and being a river pilot, and he might should have stayed there 'cause he got knocked out by Halley's Comet. Nothing has knocked me out yet.

There was the man who painted his face black and got down on one knee and sang about how much he loved his mother down on the Sewanee River. I thought it was really sweet except I thought it was really odd he had to paint his face black to love his mother. I don't remember his name either.

And the Yankee Doodle Dandy himself was here. And the man who played—oh, what was his name that slept for twenty years—he was here, not the man who slept, but the man who played him. It was a play.

There were lots of bands. The one I remember best was the one that played all the marches and the man who wrote them standing in front with his baton telling them what to do. I liked him. You could tap your feet to that music. And I could sit in the ticket office and hear that music right through the walls without having to watch the show every time. Word had it that he bent tubas into something else that was named after him, but I don't remember what that was either.

And the man who said he'd rather be here than in Philadelphia, but of course, he said that *after* he was dead. He had it carved on his tombstone. He didn't like children very much. And it was probably good that he and the woman with the ax never met each other.

And then there was a woman who had a boyfriend named Ernie. And she said—she talked about Ernie a lot and some of it was stuff that . . . Well, shut your ears if you don't want to hear it. She said, "My boyfriend Ernie and I were in bed together and he says, he say, "Soph—" I remember! Her name was Sophie. And she's talking about she and her boyfriend Ernie being in bed together. And he says, "Sophie, you got no tits, but you got a nice tight box." And she said, "Ernie! Get off my back!" The last of the red hot mamas, that's who she was. Said, "From birth to eighteen, a girl needs good parents; from eighteen to thirty-five, she needs good looks; from thirty-five to fifty-five, she needs a good personality; from fifty-five on she needs good cash. I'm saving my money." You know what she said on her eightieth birthday? "Keep breathing."

I'm more than a hundred and I'm still breathing. She didn't say what to do after a hundred. She didn't make it that far. So I sold tickets. I sold tickets to all of it. My brothers had to go off to the war—the first one, they were too old for the second—and there was nobody to sell tickets but me. I took care of tickets for more than half my life so sixty years is about right. I liked the tickets better than teaching. I didn't take much to teaching which was the other thing I could have done, it was the same old thing every day. With tickets, you met some interesting people.

I'm ready to go home now. I want to go out the front door, too.

(She is wheeled off.)

STAGE MANAGER: The woman who sold tickets mentioned—or didn't—some of the big-name people who have played on this stage: the Booths, the Barrymores, Mark Twain, Carrie A. Nation, W. C. Fields, John Philip Sousa, Sophie Tucker . . . I want to add a few more. There was The Great Zenoz, a one-legged gymnast. I have no idea what he did by way of gymnastics. There was Miss Anna Swan, the Nova Scotia Giantess. I don't know what she did, except appear on stage. She was eight feet tall. There was Wormwood's Triumphant Monkey Theatre, Trained Animal Hippodrome and Vaudeville Annex. I don't know what all they did either. What is a "Triumphant Monkey Theatre"? Then, there was The Celebrated Coleman Children Grand Juvenile Dramatic Burlesque Musical Combination and Silver Coronet Band. There were sixty-seven productions of *Uncle Tom's Cabin* here between 1866 and 1927, that's more than one a year, and the names kept getting more elaborate with each year. H. Smith's double mammoth *Uncle Tom's Cabin*. Abbey's double mammoth spectacular *Uncle Tom's Cabin*. The last one was a double with a Beethoven quartet. The touring company of *Ben-Hur* that played the Fulton had eight horses galloping abreast here at the front of the stage on treadmills for the chariot race. And the act that haunts me (not literally, there are some real haunts around here), but the performer I think of most often was a set of Siamese twins, Millie and Chrissie, the two-headed African Nightingale. They were born into slavery, bought by a man who planned to make an exhibition of them, shuffled back and forth between this country and England as the ownership of human beings got complicated. They were fused sufficiently that they could not be separated—part of their bowels were shared—and they lived until 1912, free at least, at last, from being owned, when first Chrissie, then Millie, died. They began show business as a duet act, but Millie became a hard-shell Baptist given to singing pious hymns, and Chrissie took up bawdy songs and wouldn't sing anything else. They no longer wanted to be on stage together, but they couldn't be separate either, and the act, if not the being, fell apart. Can you imagine what it meant to try to go to sleep or eat with someone so opposite, and so attached at the same time?

The Indians

BARRY: The Fulton has some ghosts, a lot of them actually. The Pennsylvania Ghost Hunters Society found more ghosts at the battlefield at Gettysburg, but they found a surprising concentration here, too. Theaters do seem to collect ghosts, and some of ours, in a specific area downstairs, were notably unhappy. How do I know that? Well, it felt awfully uncomfortable there. If you spent time in that part of the building, a storage area, you came out— "spooked" is the usual word—feeling sort of sick.

In the interest of science here—science, right!—maybe in the interest of full disclosure, the Ghost Hunters Society uses a thermometer and a digital camera for a standard photo, and infrared film in a second camera, and they take pictures of the cold spots in a place with both cameras. Things—shapes like vortexes, cones and orbs, things I could not see with my eyes—did show up on infrared film. Those, they told me, were the ghosts.

Now, before the Fulton was a theater, before it was a Civil War hospital, even before it was a community hall with a shooting gallery/beer hall upstairs and manure stocks in the basement, before all that, it was the town jail. There is a stone wall downstairs, the back wall of the present building that was part of that original jail built in 1734.

In the winter of 1763, the last fourteen of the Conestoga Indians—men, women, and children—came to that jail for their own protection. They were not prisoners; they were refugees. They were innocent of any wrongdoing and they were being pursued by the Paxton Boys, a vigilante group left over from the French and Indian Wars. On December 27, the Paxtons broke into the jail, and brutally massacred all of the Conestogas.

And the feeling was that some of the ghosts might be the spirits of those people. On June 22, 1997, we held a service for them to help their souls into the next world. It was led by Native Americans who came from across the country to do it.

Late, but better late than never.

The events in the ceremony included burning braids of sweet grass, the smoke of which is a vehicle for souls to rise to the next world, and a cleansing of bad events. It smells wonderful.

Not all of the sweet grass was used during the weekend ceremony. There was a piece left untouched that I asked if I could keep. I'm not sure why I wanted it. I can't say I planned to burn it, but I did want it, and I tossed it on top of my desk, then I locked up the office and went home. Nobody knew I had that braid except the Native American fellow I had asked for it.

Now, my whole office, desk included, is noted for being messy. Not dirty, just messy with stacks of manuscripts, books, and other stuff and nonsense of the trade—I'm playwright-in-residence here, and I have accumulated enough paper goods to make me a fire hazard unto myself. My desk is piled high with this mess. And I just added that sweet grass on top.

When I came in Monday morning, there was a path cleared from the door of my office to what was now a very clean desk. It was not a neat clearing; stacks of stuff had been pushed over onto the floor, scattered about the room, but nothing was missing, nothing destroyed. Just a path cleared, a path leading to the one thing still remaining on my desk—the braid of sweet grass.

And nobody had been here. At least, nobody we think of as alive.

I believe it was a gesture of thanks. It felt like thanks. And the area downstairs that was the jail no longer has the same collection of whatever it was that was there; it no longer felt like such an unhappy place in this building.

Barry Kornhauser, the source of The Indians *story, is playwright-in-residence at the Fulton. He also helped with the history of the Fulton, from which I wrote the ticket-taker character (the Woman) and the piece* Old. *I selected my details, Barry knew the history far better than the ticket taker remembered it.*

Geology

Walton County, Florida

THE DIVER: This is an amazing place. There is the beach, the Emerald Coast, and that is what gets the tourists. But this is one of two places in the world—the other is on the east coast of Africa—that has freshwater lakes from springs right behind the dunes of the saltwater gulf. One of two.

We sit at the downhill end of a huge aquifer here. The east of this country, and maybe more, is drained here. We're on limestone which is water soluble, and the water runs through the aquifer underground and comes to surface. Here. It comes in some pretty amazing ways.

DeFuniak Springs is one such place. What you see on the surface is a little lake, about a mile in circumference with no outlet. Sixty feet below the surface, in the center, is a spring that is at an equilibrium with the lake it creates. The lake rises or falls with drier or wetter weather, but the lake stays, loses its water by evaporation.

Early, it was a scared place for the Indians. Then it was a watering hole for the whites. Now it is the fashion in DeFuniak Springs to have a house on the Circle Drive around the lake.

Not far away is Ponce De Leon Spring, now a state park and recreation area, also a place where water emerges from this aquifer.

But the spring I want to talk about, because it is the one I've been in, is Morrison Spring.

First time we went to dive there, the water was high, and we drove into it before we realized it. Almost flooded the engine of the car. Would have if we hadn't been in a rear-engine Volkswagen. It was that clear. It is surrounded by an old cypress forest. If the water is low, you see the cypress' knees. If the water is high, you can be in it before you know you are. It is bigger than DeFuniak Spring, bigger than Ponce, there are no houses in the cypress forest, no state recreation area with designated swimming areas. It is private property and you can swim at your own risk for a small fee . . .

And we—always dive with a buddy—decided to dive. We'd been there and seen other people diving. The astronauts used to come there from Cape Canaveral, something to do with time off, and go diving. So we went.

At Morrison, you can swim out and look down and see where the spring is with sixty feet of water above it. It is a hole about eight feet in diameter and water comes out of it fast. Millions of gallons a day. You can see it bubbling up at the surface sixty feet above the hole. We put on the gear and went down.

What was hard about the dive was getting in that opening at all. You can't swim against that much pressure, you have to find handholds in a stone tube that water has been washing the handholds out of for thousands of years. You have to pull yourself along against the current of the water, about fifteen, maybe twenty feet.

It opens into a huge cavern below the hole, about a hundred and fifty feet long. Now you're in the dark, in a cave with water flowing through it fast. What you don't know going in, is where all water flows out of this cavern. There may be even bigger places than the opening you came in where water continues to flow underground.

And you do not want to try to go out anywhere at all but where you came in.

So you mark where you came in.

You don't just mark it, it is not like you are carrying a piece of chalk and draw a little arrow on the wall. You anchor one end of a string, we usually keep about a half a mile of builder's string, the strong nylon stuff, and you roll out the string as you go. That way, even if you lose your light, you can still get out. Assuming the string doesn't break. That's one of the ways people die in these places. These are dangerous places.

The string did not break this dive. We got into the first big cavern, and what we were trying to do was move against the flow of the water to find where it comes into that cavern. We found it, this one was a much easier passage, we were in another good-sized cavern, and following the flow of water in it, and we got to a tube the water was coming through. There was not enough room in the tube for a diver with the air tanks on, so you take the tanks off, still breathing from them, and push them ahead of you through this tube. This was about eight feet of really hard going, again, because you are trying to move against the pressure of so much water. But we did that, too, into another cavern, and at that point, we still had lots of string, but not a lot of air, and we were about two hundred and fifty feet underground. That's as deep as you can go in water without decompressing on the way out. And it is a lot faster on the way out whether you want it to be or not, because you are going with the flow instead of against it. So we followed the string out, found the opening that led to the surface and came to air again.

Now I spend the time on this geology because it is what this place is, limestone that we live on and build houses on and make roads on and go to the grocery store on, but under those houses and grocery stores, under the sushi bars and tourist traps, and not very far under it, one of the biggest aquifers on the continent runs through caverns and chutes, runs from tremendous pressure behind it, runs to the surface of the ground and into the sea.

———

Dick McCrite is the diver who told me about going into Morrison Springs.

Plowing Outback

Newport News, Virginia

Three people come to an outside table at a restaurant. The Waitperson attends to them.

WAITPERSON: Thank you for choosing to dine with us. My name is _____, I'll be your waitperson this evening. Our specials tonight are . . . *(Doesn't matter what is said here, it just needs to be inaudible and said in a singsong voice)* and our desserts are so big no single person can eat all of one of them and our pies are just like homemade. Now, what can I bring you to drink?

(Two of the people deal with the Waitperson.)

THIRD PERSON: This was once a field I plowed. I mean this table, this restaurant sits on land I used to plow. My father before me plowed it, too, raised silage for cows. The business was a dairy, but cows have to be fed. Food is cheaper to raise than to buy.

My father used to say if you waited for perfect weather to plow, it would never get done. He was speaking of this field, but he was speaking to a son who was bad about putting things off. I didn't understand until it was me deciding when to plow this field, and, of course, I said it to my son who never had the opportunity or the obligation to plow this field, never had to make the decision about when to plow, so never had the bone learning that comes of sitting on a tractor dragging a plow, because the time is right even if conditions aren't.

Once, my father was plowing this field and a salesman showed up. He wasn't much of a man to talk to salesmen to begin with, and he was busy. Plowing Cheddar's. Plowing Office Max. Plowing JC Penney. Plowing Outback's. Plowing outback. The salesman came into the field—the gate was over close to where ToysЯUs is now—stood there waiting while my father drove the tractor with the plow behind it around the whole field, it was a big field, through Barnes & Noble, through Don Pablo's Mexican Restaurant, through the mall, could be forty-five minutes once around, and the salesman started waving when he got close, and my father waved back and kept on. Man was still there when he came around again. My father waved again and kept on again. Salesman gave up. My father plowed until after sunset by the lights on the tractor to get it done. Next day, you do the same thing with a disk to break up clods and then you can plant. You drive the tractor around again to harvest. After the zoning changed and taxes got high, it was me being plowed. This restaurant should be named Progress. Selling the land was not an option. I had to. I don't begrudge people homes and a way of life. I don't begrudge it at all, and heavens knows, I got fair trade for the land. And so many more people live here now. Things cannot stay the same, and I can't make them, don't want to. I even like good restaurants. But sometimes I do miss the gentle, sisterly company of those cows.

Other Places

Cambodia

WOMAN: I like much better to talk about now. I am a wife, a mother of three daughters. My daughters go to bed at nine o'clock, and I make sure they have their homework done. I coach my oldest daughter's soccer team, I play volleyball. I keep house. I help my husband. We have a small business. He is from here. We are very happy.

I am from Cambodia.

There is a lot of this I have very little memory of because I spent so many years too tired to remember much, and too hungry to care.

When I was about the age of my second daughter (eight, nine), my parents and I were forced into a work camp by the Khmer Rouge. There was not enough food. The old and the weak were shot. When they had used us till we were dying, they lined us up to be shot. And I ran.

I was about the age of my oldest daughter. She is eleven.

Soldiers chased me but they missed me. I ran over a mountain and into another valley and into another work camp. I, and other people, escaped from that one and went into Thailand to a refugee camp, but, after a few months, Thailand decided we had to go back, and they put us on busses. There were thirteen busses that started. Two returned. The rest were blown up by mines. There were bodies everywhere but not mine, I lived through that, too. With some others, I went to Vietnam, to Hanoi. I met my grandparents there, but they were worse off than I was, and the police come to get me—I was sleeping anywhere I could—to try to put me in another refugee camp. So I ran from them, too, and went back to Cambodia. But there was nothing there to eat, and I went back to Thailand, to another refugee camp. The Red Cross fed people there. By then, I was fifteen and I had spent eight years in one camp or another and or running away through jungles, through rivers, over mountains.

I have lived through bombs, I have lived through the middle of battles. I have been shot at many times, I was almost starved, I had almost drowned many times, and I was alone. I lived only because I did not want to die. There certainly wasn't much to live for.

And from that refugee camp, they said I could come to the United States. March 27, 1982. The agency sent me to a foster family in New York, and I stayed there for two years, a little more, and then I come here. And taking a taxi here, I met who was going to be my husband. After three dates he said he wanted to marry me. I made him wait five months. I was not going to marry somebody I didn't know. We are very happy.

Greece

Lancaster, Pennsylvania

MOTHER: I met my husband in college, he was in seminary, and he was assigned to the church here. That is how I came here. We've been happy here. Thirty-six years.

SON: That's her short answer to the question about how she came to be here. This woman has another answer. I know her. I am her son.

MOTHER: Everybody came from somewhere else sometime . . .

SON: Mother, you come from the most amazing story I know. Her father, my grandfather came to this country when he was eleven, from a very poor island in Greece. He went to school at night and worked as a dishwasher. He became a cook, and he eventually opened his own restaurant. When it came time to marry, he went back to Greece for a bride, and brought back a woman who was homesick from the day she got here.

MOTHER: She never learned English. Life was hard for her here. But life had been hard in Greece, too, and she wasn't hungry here. My father was a good provider.

SON: They had four children, and right before World War II broke out, she decided she wanted to go home for a visit, and if the coming war—

MOTHER: Nobody spoke of the "coming war." They just knew Europe was tense, and my mother wanted to see her parents again desperately, and if war did break out, who knew how long it would be before she could? She wanted her children to meet them and know them. And she was so homesick. So it was agreed, my father agreed, we would all go except him.

SON: So my grandmother took her children, my mother was one of them, to meet their grandparents and left her husband in America to run his restaurant. Where was he then?

MOTHER: New Jersey. He had family there. His father and some aunts lived there.

SON: And the war broke out while Grandmother and my mother and her three brothers were in Greece, and they could not come home. You need to be the one telling this . . .

MOTHER: My grandparents were poor people. Everyone was poor, at least where we were on that island, and my grandparents were no different. They lived in a tiny village and kept goats, and had a vegetable patch, and, even before the war, five extra mouths to feed were a real burden.

SON: And when Italy went with the Axis, Italy invaded Greece. Greece didn't have much for an army, and the Italians occupied Greece . . .

MOTHER: Italians, yes, such conquerors, but with the Italians came their allies. The Germans were a different story. My grandparents lost most of what they had to the Germans, and there was not enough food at all, and my mother moved us to a fishing village, thinking that the ocean, at least, has food in it. Easier food to get. And maybe it was a little easier, but not much. And then, back in the first village, my grandfather was killed over a goat he used for milk that a soldier wanted to make a meal of, and Mother invited Grandmother to come live with us, and she did. There were six of us.

Until the war, we had been getting money from my father, but when the war started, mail didn't come anymore. The man who owned the house we were in let us stay there anyway. And, again, there was not enough food. My oldest brother was ten. He spoke English and Greek, and he found he could beg, and make his own way as a translator, and he spent most of the war in Athens on his own. My next older brother was sent into the mountains with the sheepherders, men who had been friends of my grandfather, and he spent the war there.

SON: My uncles have their own stories.

MOTHER: They do. But we were still starving. And my mother had a friend, a woman she had been close to growing up who had lost a daughter, and who offered to take me. They had food. I did not want to leave my mother, I was seven years old, I didn't want to go with someone I didn't know, but my brothers had been brave, and there was no real choice, and I was sent off. My mother and I were both crying. She still had another child to feed . . .

SON: Now, the Italians had overrun the Greek army, but overrunning the Greeks was another problem. There was an underground. Guerrillas.

MOTHER: And the husband of the woman who took me in was a guerrilla.

SON: He used my mother to send messages.

MOTHER: I was a child, I could do things an adult could not do. I never knew what was in the messages, I just knew who I was supposed to take them to, and I knew that if a German tried to catch me, I was to tear the piece of paper up and throw it away before I got caught. These were tiny little squares of paper—even paper was hard to come by—I was to chew it up and swallow it if I could. I did this for a year, maybe a little more.

SON: And she got caught.

MOTHER: They did not get the message. I don't know what it said, but the Germans didn't get it.

SON: They got her. They put her in a prison camp. What were you, eight?

MOTHER: Maybe nine by then. They considered me dangerous because of the guerrillas. The Germans said for every

German that was killed, they would kill twenty of the Greeks, whoever they came to first, it didn't matter, and they did that, but it did not stop the guerrillas.

SON: And they tortured you for information.

MOTHER: They made me watch executions. But I didn't know anything. There was nothing to get from me. They shot friends of mine, young men in the village who had been nice to me, and they made me watch, thinking I was going to be next. They shot the man who needed me to carry messages.

I got very, very sick. I was too cold, even in the heat of summer, and I could not get warm. I was sure I would never see my mother or my brothers again, I was sure I wouldn't live, and I didn't want to, and my body was accommodating me. And then, the Germans found out I wasn't Greek, I was American—America hadn't entered the war yet—and they dumped me out of the prison camp and back to the woman who had taken me in. But now her husband was dead, and she had no more food than anybody else.

I didn't get any warmer at all, and there are no medicines for cold. They warmed bricks and wrapped them in rags and put them next to my body. I didn't even feel it, one burnt me and I didn't know. It was a bad burn. I was dying. An old woman, a woman who said she had "nothing to live for, and so nothing to lose," decided to take me and try to find my mother. Nobody knew if she was still alive, many were not by then, but the old woman thought if she could find her, I might have some reason to live again. I remember riding a donkey over mountains. I don't remember much of it. I do know the donkey had been hard to find—he was valuable to the guerrillas and everyone else—so we spent a lot of our time hiding. The old woman used her body to cover me, her body heat for mine, she opened her clothes and wrapped me against her body and carried me like that, sometimes both of us on the donkey. And she found my mother.

I do not know that woman's name. I do not know whether she survived the war. I don't even know if she survived the trip home. But she delivered me to my mother, and turned around, and climbed back on that donkey, and rode away.

And I got warm again.

SON: One of the miracles of this story is that all of them lived, lived to come home on the second boat that left Greece after the war, lived to be met by the man who loved them, and had missed them terribly and worried and prayed for them. He wanted them all to kiss the earth of this country, he begged them to do that, and they did.

MOTHER: I was eleven when we got back, I had no formal education, I spoke Greek, not English anymore, and I had been to hell. My father forbade us to even speak of our experiences, he wanted us to forget; he wanted us not to have lived through that experience. He wanted us to behave as if we hadn't even been there. None of us even knew him anymore, and he didn't know us. My mother was a frightened shadow of herself, and we were wild children. They put me into first grade with six year olds. "Dick and Jane" and "See Spot run" after I had watched my friends executed. They sent my older brothers to military school "for some discipline" they said. My brothers did not adapt as well as I did, but it was not easy for me.

And there was always the threat that my parents' fragile marriage would break apart. My mother never did learn to speak English. I reconciled myself to staying at home, because, when I was there, I was a buffer between them, but my oldest brother insisted that I go to college. I earned my own way—my father had paid for my brothers to go but he didn't think a girl needed an education—so I felt obliged.

And while I was at college, with no time at all between jobs and studies, I met a young seminarian who did not shy away from my questions about the goodness of man or God, or the things I had seen in my life, who wanted to marry me, and I said yes. He was assigned here. We decided we'd try it, move on if we didn't like it. We've been here thirty-six years.

This is my youngest of four children, he is a priest himself now, and he is the one who went back to Greece with me to revisit the places I remembered, and he is the one who thought I should tell the story of what happened to me before I came here.

———

Lancaster, Pennsylvania, is a city of tremendous diversity. We set out to represent some of that in the play we did. This story and the Cambodian Woman's story were part of that endeavor.

The Countess

Newport News, Virginia

Joe Burke's office. Joe's Secretary is a refugee.

JOE: Miss Zook . . .

>   *(Joe's Secretary pays no attention, she does not answer.)*

>   Miss Zook . . .

>   *(Same. They've been through this before.)*

You're going to have to quit this.

SECRETARY: You know, I'll answer if you address me properly.

JOE: I will not call you by a title. I will not.

SECRETARY: I had a pillow in my bed that had been my mother's before she died, it still smelled faintly of lavender because she rinsed her hair in lavender water. And that was home. I slept in a bed that was carved by my grandfather from the trunk of a single tree. He did it because he liked to work in wood, not because he was good at it. The bed was askew, but it was home. On the wall of my bedroom was a painting by my crazy Aunt Katrine, the least crazy woman I've ever known. She was married to a hard man much older than she, and when she'd had enough of him, she would quit talking, and he'd send her to a very expensive, lovely sanitarium to recover. She would practice her skills as a painter. It was a new fashion in therapy at that place. Her paintings looked down the throats of flowers. Her therapist would talk about how it was an expression of her need to "go inside" and not speak, and they were stunning, exotic paintings. What hung on my wall of my room was the view down the throat of a white lily. At the bottom was a tiny cross like it was part of the flower with Christ hanging on it. That painting hung on my wall instead of the usual crucifix. I could get lost in that painting. And that was home. Our house was on property that had been in my family for two hundred years. I knew every field of it. And that was home. The farm was on a road, and I knew every one up and down, both directions, both sides. And that was home. Russia was home—the wheat in the fields, the great horses, the language I spoke was home, the air, the rain (when it came), the winters of snow . . .

And none of that, none of it, none, is here.

The only things I have here are the things that cannot be taken away without taking my life, too, and my title is one of them. I was born to it. You must call me "Countess," you have to, it is what I have left of home.

JOE: You have your voice. You sing like an angel . . .

SECRETARY: Mr. Joe Burke Who Does His Service, I have heard your saying about "singing for your supper" but I have not yet found a place where I can do that. I must "type" for my supper instead. I suppose I should be glad I have some supper to type for. Yes?

———

This is from a play called Hand-Me-Down Shoes. *The play was written for the Mennonite community in Newport News, Virginia, right after 9/11, by way of a response. The Mennonite idea of response is, needless to say, different from the George W. Bush idea. The main story in the play concerns a*

Mennonite man, Joe Burke, who did his service in Constantinople (now Istanbul) right after World War I. The Mennonites have a tradition of service all over the world. The service is not proselytizing in intent, it is just to go where you are needed and stay till the job is done. This was just one such story. But it was an appropriate story because Joe Burke was witness to (and wrote home about) some of "the insult of eighty years ago" mentioned in Osama Bin Laden's post-9/11 video.

Prior to World War I, the religious leader of the Ottoman Empire had also been its political leader. The Allied victors (the Ottoman Empire had fought on Germany's side) forced a change and broke up the Ottoman Empire, and at the time of Joe Burke's service, this deposed leader was allowed to go to the mosque only once a week, on Friday afternoon, to pray. It must have been quite a parade between his guards and the people who wanted him restored to his previous position.

In the meantime, the revolution in Russia was beginning, and most of the refugees Joe Burke was serving were people who had fled Russia with the downfall of the czar. The secretary in this piece is one of those people. Joe called her "Miss Zook" in his letters, but it is probably a shortening of her real name. Joe's job was distributing clothes to these Russian people, many who did not consider Mennonite fashion quite up to their standards. For instance, Joe was troubled when a woman spit on what he considered a perfectly good, if somewhat worn, winter coat. The second wave of refugees that came to Constantinople during Joe Burke's service was very different. These were mostly other Mennonites, descendants of people who had settled on the steppes of Russia a hundred years before at the invitation of Catherine the Great. They were excellent farmers but they were an insular community, and most spoke German and hadn't learned Russian (even though it was a hundred years and some generations later). Germany had been an enemy of Russia during World War I, Russia fought with the Allies. These Mennonites were subjected to terrible brutalities by a group of vigilantes who would eventually join the Red Army but were called, at the time, the Anarchists. Mennonites are pacifist, fighting was an offense against God. They were being murdered, but, if, in desperation, they resorted to self-defense, the Anarchists became even more brutal. Many had lost their families and all had lost their farms and their animals, and they fled two thousand miles or more on foot to get to Joe Burke's line of refugees; they were people truly in need of a used coat and hand-me-down shoes. Joe Burke's service had real value.

Every person in the play is missing home and the safety of home, even Joe Burke, and many are from homes that proved terribly unsafe. Miss Zook's evocation of what home is happens early in the play and sets a theme.

Troubles and Fears

Brown Dress

Colquitt, Georgia

This piece is played by a black woman and a white woman as if they were one person. The Police Officer can be any race.
The Officer is taking notes, a deposition.

BOTH WOMEN: He bought me a brown dress.
WHITE WOMAN: It was a house dress kind of thing,
BLACK WOMAN: cheap and flimsy and too big for me, and it was my Easter dress.
WHITE WOMAN: He dressed like a peacock,
BLACK WOMAN: hundred-dollar suits, and good shirts and shoes. He wore
WHITE WOMAN: three shirts a day, and he wanted them blue-white,
BLACK WOMAN: starched and ironed,
WHITE WOMAN: and I spent my Saturdays on them,
BLACK WOMAN: twenty-one a week. Not to mention mine and the children's clothes. I was ironing shirts
WHITE WOMAN: when he came in with this dress.
BLACK WOMAN: I wouldn't have worn it to teach school.
WHITE WOMAN: I didn't.

BLACK WOMAN: It is still hanging in my closet.

WHITE WOMAN: I wore it once.

BOTH WOMEN: That Easter Sunday.

BLACK WOMAN: I didn't say a word about it. I was supposed to be

WHITE WOMAN: thankful for it.

BLACK WOMAN: He told me

WHITE WOMAN: I better act thankful for it

BOTH WOMEN: even if I wasn't.

WHITE WOMAN: Looking at it made me cry, not just the dress, but the threat of it. All the threat. And his sisters

BLACK WOMAN: out prowling on the road for footprints

WHITE WOMAN: to see if I'd walked anywhere when he wasn't there. Every day,

BLACK WOMAN: they'd get out on the road and look and see if my footprints were there.

WHITE WOMAN: Sometimes they were. We have a car,

BLACK WOMAN: but if the children and I weren't ready when he thought we ought to be,

WHITE WOMAN: he'd drive away and leave us

BOTH WOMEN: and there was hell to pay

BLACK WOMAN: if we weren't where we were to go on time.

BOTH WOMEN: He and I worked in the same place,

WHITE WOMAN: and the children went to school there,

BOTH WOMEN: we went to the same church,

BLACK WOMAN: but I can't tell you how often we walked and he didn't.

WHITE WOMAN: And those sisters, they'd say,

BLACK WOMAN: "She's been out . . ."

WHITE WOMAN: "She's been out . . ."

BLACK WOMAN: "She's been out . . ."

BOTH WOMEN: ". . . walking, Brother."

WHITE WOMAN: And then, he'd want to know where I'd been.

BLACK WOMAN: To church. On Easter Sunday

BOTH WOMEN: in a trashy brown dress.

WHITE WOMAN: It wasn't just the dress.

OFFICER: Can you get to the night in question, please.

WHITE WOMAN: There are fourteen years of nights in question,

BLACK WOMAN: almost all in which he did something to me or the children,

WHITE WOMAN: and one

BLACK WOMAN: in which I did something

WHITE WOMAN: to him. Now, I know what you want me to say, and I'm getting to it, but I'm not going to say it without this . . . and what I really want to know is why you've not been here before now.

BLACK WOMAN: 'Cause I'm black and what happens in this neighborhood is not something you worry much about?

WHITE WOMAN: Because this time it is a man that's been hurt and not a woman?

OFFICER: I got a call, ma'am.

WHITE WOMAN: I know you did. I'm the one who called you. I don't care if you don't write down about the dress, but write this down.

BOTH WOMEN: He beat us, all of us.

WHITE WOMAN: His sisters saw that, too, but they didn't worry about that.

BLACK WOMAN: They were here, both of them, the nights all three of my children were born, and they'd look at those babies when they came out of my body and try to decide whether or not they looked like him.

WHITE WOMAN: They were his, all of them.

BLACK WOMAN: He beat me the night the third one was born because they didn't think she looked like him.

WHITE WOMAN: And he beat her.

BLACK WOMAN: Not that night, but as she grew. She's nine years old and she has scars all over her back where her clothes cover them and you can't see them.

WHITE WOMAN: He is careful about that. I've got scars on my back, too.

BOTH WOMEN: We all do. And then he takes a deacon's job in church. And he's principal at the school.

WHITE WOMAN: A fine man,

BLACK WOMAN: a real role model.

WHITE WOMAN: He beat everything that could be hurt by beating

BLACK WOMAN: except those sisters of his.

WHITE WOMAN: Now, did you write that down?

OFFICER: Victim allegedly beat wife and children.

(The White Woman jerks the tail of her blouse from her skirt and holds it up to show the Officer her back.)

Jesus, woman, looks like you've been worked over with a bullwhip.

WHITE WOMAN: I have been. "Victim BEAT his wife and children." Mark out "allegedly."

OFFICER: It's just the legal language.

BLACK WOMAN: Mark it out.

OFFICER: It's out. *(Writes something else)*

BLACK WOMAN: He kept a gun in his coat pocket.

WHITE WOMAN: Loaded.

BLACK WOMAN: A .38.

WHITE WOMAN: And a shotgun in the house.

BLACK WOMAN: Also loaded. And when he came in this afternoon, he took his coat off—

WHITE WOMAN: it was hot—

BLACK WOMAN: and for no reason that I know—he hauled the youngest into our room. I could hear her screaming.

WHITE WOMAN: And I don't know why it was this day and not some other, but I said to myself, Enough is enough.

BLACK WOMAN: Enough is enough. I didn't see his coat, I figured he still had the .38 in his pocket.

WHITE WOMAN: I thought,

BLACK WOMAN: I might die but I've thought that before and I didn't. So I walked into our room

WHITE WOMAN: and pointed the shotgun at him and told him quit

BLACK WOMAN: or I'd shoot him,

WHITE WOMAN: and he came after me.

BLACK WOMAN: He felt

WHITE WOMAN: for his gun, I saw him

BLACK WOMAN: and I ran into the yard. I was yelling for help when he came out the door

WHITE WOMAN: and he had his coat in his hand and he was reaching for the gun in the pocket of it,

BLACK WOMAN: and I pointed the shotgun at him and I pulled the trigger

BOTH WOMEN: and he fell on the porch and died.

BLACK WOMAN: I killed him.

WHITE WOMAN: There are the words you're looking for. Write them down.

BLACK WOMAN: Now. Read me what you've written.

WHITE WOMAN: I am an English teacher.

OFFICER: Brown dress.

BLACK WOMAN: Cross out "brown dress."

WHITE WOMAN: It is not a complete sentence. And it doesn't matter.

OFFICER: Suspect states victim beat her and their children. Suspect states a beating of youngest child was in process. Suspect states she had reason to believe victim was armed. Suspect states she tried to halt beating. Suspect states she shot victim in self-defense.

BLACK WOMAN: "Suspect." And that's it?

WHITE WOMAN: That's all you wrote of what I told you?

OFFICER: That's all I need.

BLACK WOMAN: But it is not the story.

WHITE WOMAN: That is not nearly the story.

(The Officer exits. The two women straighten, collect themselves, stand as if they were speaking to a jury, testifying.)

BLACK WOMAN: I am not proud of this story,

BOTH WOMEN: not the least bit proud

WHITE WOMAN: of what I did,

BLACK WOMAN: but I did it, I did do it,

WHITE WOMAN: and I would do it again tomorrow if I had to,

BLACK WOMAN: and my regret, if I have one

WHITE WOMAN: is that I did not do it sooner . . . my children
BLACK WOMAN: my children must forgive me
WHITE WOMAN: first for living with him
BLACK WOMAN: and then, for murdering him.
WHITE WOMAN: And both those things
BLACK WOMAN: are very hard to forgive . . .

This piece was from one woman in the oral history as it came to me. She was known in the community; she'd stood trial and had been acquitted. But by the time I saw this story, I had some experience with abuse stories and I'd found that they are all too easily dismissed. We're really bad, seeing just what we want to see and no more, and nobody wants to see this, especially not in their own neighborhood. So my director, Richard Geer, and I decided we'd try something different. I wrote it for two women to tell the same story: one black, one white, so at the very least, in its second life on stage, this story wouldn't be identifiable by race. Race is, unfortunately, one of the easier ways to dismiss hard stories. And writing it for a black woman and a white woman suggests that abuse doesn't just happen in one community or the other. This story has gone on to have a considerable second life, either revised as a monologue or— mostly—as written.

It has been used regularly in south Georgia to raise money for women's shelters. And my doctor and I have used this and other stories to help people affected by abuse in my East Tennessee community. She was seeing a lot of abuse come through her examining room, and real stories are more compelling than numbers and analysis. We spoke as a team, to raise money for women's shelters. We went to medical conferences, medical classrooms, psychology classrooms, anywhere that wanted us, and a few places that, after they'd heard what we had to say, didn't. One time we were even told, "You really shouldn't tell stories like that. It's very upsetting." I was reminded of Flannery O'Connor's tired reader who wanted to be uplifted (from her essay "Some Aspects of the Grotesque in Southern Fiction," from Mystery and Manners*). My doctor's numbers suggested that maybe as many as one out of seven people (mostly women, but not exclusively) who came through her examining room had likely experienced some kind of abuse. And most wouldn't talk about it. They were afraid to. Now, it is a very self-selected group, people who go to the doctor on any given day, but the number alone is reason for telling such a story as this one.*

Whipping

Newport News, Virginia

YOUNG MAN: The last whipping I ever got was a whipping
I gave. I was about thirteen, I had been messing with the
battery setup at the barn. I knew I wasn't supposed to, and
worse, I had fouled the works. I knew I was in for a whip-
ping, too. My father sent me out to get my own switch. And
when I brought it back in, I tried to hand it to him. He said:
"No, you're going to whip me."
"I can't do that."
"Yes, you can."
And he bent over. I couldn't do it.
"Hit me."
"I don't want to."
"Do it."
He made me whip him, like he would have whipped me.
It took a long time because I didn't want to, but he wouldn't
let me go without really doing it. I was crying worse than
if I was being whipped. I've never done anything since that
made me feel so bad. I threw up and he still wouldn't let me
quit. When he finally stood up he said:
"How does that make you feel?"
"Awful."

"That's how I feel every time I have to whip you. So, please, don't do things that make me have to do it . . . "

———

I've seen a lot of stories that include whippings. A few are in this book. Whippings were the fashion in child-raising for a very long time. And there are plenty of people now who will tell you that some child or other would be far better off for an occasional whipping. I've been in situations when I wished an indulgent parent would try something different. (I know I've wished I could tie a specific teenager to her bed or the toilet or somewhere, even for just a few minutes, to ensure that she wasn't leaving out the back window of her bedroom. Again.) So I understand how angry a person can get, how difficult it can be. But my feeling is that inflicting calculated pain and humiliation, like a whipping, is never a good idea. Such violence begets, at the very least, mistrust and ill will. At the worst, violence begets more and more violence. I still remember how irresolvably angry the whippings I got made me. So I'm not an advocate of whipping anything—adult or child or animal—as a means of control or as punishment. (I've seen some bad horse trainers, too, that is why I include animals.) I find this story to be the most astonishing use of a whipping of any I ever came across, and I pass it along for the shock value. Those moments that most confound our expectations are sometimes the moments in which we learn the most.

Somewhere Safe

Newport News, Virginia

A WOMAN: I may have been six, and I had been warned not to play with matches, that they were not toys and that I could hurt myself with them. But I watched my mother put a box of matches away in the pantry, and I climbed up on a chair after her and got a handful of them. I took them out between the house and the barn and I struck them, all of them at once, they made a huge flame in my hand and I got very frightened and I pulled my hand into my side. I put the flame out with that gesture, but I made a burn on my side, the scar of it is still there.

My father found me, crying, evidence of what I had done at my feet, the burn in my dress and my side. He didn't get mad, but he explained that what I had done was very dangerous, that fire could go everywhere, especially if there was something like kerosene to help spread it. We had kerosene in the barn, I knew we did.

Everywhere. I thought about our house. We could go to the barn if the house caught fire, except if fire went everywhere, the barn was part of everywhere.

We could go to our neighbor's house. But that was part of everywhere.

We could go to the church, to the school, but that too was part of everywhere.

I lay in bed that night, my side still hurt with the burn, and tried to think of somewhere that wasn't part of everywhere.

That night and many, many more nights, long after the burn had healed.

It was the problem of my childhood. It became my obsession, to think of the somewhere that wasn't part of the everywhere a fire could go.

Somewhere safe.

In the way of children, I did think of a place. I had been to Maryland once to visit my grandfather, and we could go to his house. It was far enough away that maybe it wasn't part of the everywhere my father spoke about, it was in another state and surely fire couldn't go there . . . If fire came, we would go to Maryland.

But I knew better, I could tell myself Granddaddy's house was safe during the day, but in my dreams at night, fire came to Maryland, too . . .

Covet

Colquitt, Georgia

This is played by five women. They are at a graveside under umbrellas; it is a funeral in the rain. They begin facing the grave. They turn to face the audience when they have lines, then turn back to the grave again when they are through. Sometimes, two or more of them face out, sometimes they speak to each other across the solitude of the umbrellas, but the point of the umbrellas is to isolate each of them.

WOMAN 1: I was five. What can you covet when you are five years old? Your older sister's new shoes?

WOMAN 2: But you had new shoes, too. Barely used, shoes she had outgrown, but new to you. And you had no need of fancy shoes.

WOMAN 1: I had work to do.

WOMAN 2: Everybody had work to do.

WOMAN 1: I had to carry water.

WOMAN 3: Are you going to pass his house again?

WOMAN 1: I carried a bucket at a time, because I was not big enough to carry two buckets, and I had to pass his house to do it.

WOMAN 4: And what did he covet?

WOMAN 1: I don't care.

WOMAN 4: You do, you care very much.

WOMAN 1: I'm glad he is dead.

WOMAN 2: I know. I hate funerals.

WOMAN 3: I know. I am always back at his funeral and I am ten years old, and the minute I am let out of this church, out from behind my mother's skirt, my mother who doesn't know anything, who doesn't want to know anything, especially when I give her some of those quarters.

WOMAN 1: I will run and scream and play with the others. There is no greater joy for any of us than his death, and this day is our . . .

WOMAN 4: Redemption?

WOMAN 1: Oh, I wish, but it isn't. It is just a release, no more.

WOMAN 3: Is it a sin to be so glad he died?

WOMAN 1: I can't help it if it is.

WOMAN 4: You have to stand here anyway. We all have to stand here. He was a deacon here. Everybody in the church comes to his funeral.

WOMAN 1: So I look at Sara, Alice, Jane and Morgan, a girl named Morgan.

WOMAN 4: Do the others look back?

WOMAN 1: No. But they know I'm looking at them, and they know I am one of them. Each of us knows the other is one of us.

WOMAN 4: How would they know?

WOMAN 1: They suspect like I suspect, they know like I know. We each saw the other coming out of his house. It was a shack, it wasn't a house. You could smell it, the unwashed clothes, unchanged bedding, and too many times he just went in the yard when he was too lazy to get to the outhouse.

WOMAN 5: "A good man has fallen on hard times."

WOMAN 4: Daddy said that.

WOMAN 3: Daddy didn't know any better either.

WOMAN 2: Daddy didn't want to know any better.

WOMAN 1: I think sometimes about people who punish themselves somehow, sometimes really badly, because they think they are sinners.

WOMAN 5: Are you one of them?

WOMAN 1: I think I am.

WOMAN 5: Was he?

WOMAN 1: He had money. I mean, he had plenty of quarters when he wanted them. But he lived in such squalor. Why else, except to punish himself, why else would he live with such filth?

WOMAN 5: What did he covet?

WOMAN 1: He would watch me when I passed his house.

WOMAN 5: He said, "Come here."

WOMAN 2: No.

WOMAN 5: "Come over here, I've got a present for you."

WOMAN 1: A present. I would like very much to have a present.

WOMAN 5: So you wanted a present. Your first present was a doll with an eye poked out.

WOMAN 1: But that was ok, I could find a pretty rock to go in the eyehole. Except I remember where he touched me before he gave it to me. *(She touches her chest)*

WOMAN 2: You had no . . .

WOMAN 1: I had a child's body. I was five years old. I had a tooth missing and white chicken fuzz for hair, and I prided myself on how fast I could run. I was so fast. He wanted to touch a child. My second present was a quarter.

WOMAN 2: A quarter was a lot of money then.

WOMAN 1: I had never had a quarter of my own before. I coveted that quarter. And his hand was not pleasant, but it was a sort of caress and it didn't hurt . . . He hurt Sara. She had to pass his house, too. I saw her coming out, and she was crying.

WOMAN 5: "Come here. I'm lonely."

WOMAN 1: He gave her quarters, too. She wanted the quarters just like I did. A quarter was so much money.

WOMAN 5: What did he covet?

WOMAN 2: Why do you keep asking that? I don't care. He was a pervert. He hurt Jane, too. I don't know about Alice and Morgan.

WOMAN 5: Are you are free because he is dead?

WOMAN 1: I want this funeral to be over, I want to run like the child I could have been in the yard. I want all of us to run—

Sara and Alice and Jane and Morgan—and look one another
in the eyes and know he is not in that house anymore.

WOMAN 5: "Come here. You are so pretty, little girl. So pretty,
you have white hair."

WOMAN 1: What's wrong with wanting a quarter?

WOMAN 3: My mother never told me a word until after I got
my period, and when it came I thought I might be dying.
All she said was that it was natural and, "You must not let
any boys touch you."

WOMAN 2: But the dispenser of quarters wasn't a boy. And by
the time he started doing the things that hurt, I was guilty,
too. Guilty of the pleasure of those quarters, and I didn't
know how to say no.

WOMAN 5: "Here, girlie, you're big enough now to climb up
here and sit on my lap."

WOMAN 1: Please. Stop it.

WOMAN 3: It will be forty years before you can tell this story,
even to yourself.

WOMAN 1: I want to run in the yard.

WOMAN 2: Forty years before I can stand at anyone's funeral,
even someone I love, without reliving this funeral.

WOMAN 1: I want us to look one another in the eyes and know
he isn't there.

WOMAN 4: Forty years before I begin to wonder what happened
to us, and if they ever spoke to anyone, and if they are afraid
of funerals, too.

WOMAN 1: I want to look them in the eyes, and know we do not
have to pass by that house ever again.

WOMAN 4: Forty years before you can say to yourself why you
are so fearful.

WOMAN 1: I want to run. I want to go outside and run. I am so
fast when I run, it is very hard to see me when I run.

WOMAN 5: Forty years in the wilderness.

(They all turn back to the funeral.)

Ashes to ashes, dust to dust . . .

Covet *is another story that my director, Richard Geer, and I did not want to be age- or class- or race-specific. The players ranged in age from twelve to sixty in all the color varieties that could be found. It was Richard Geer who thought to give them all separate umbrellas to speak of their isolation.*

Covet Follow-Up
(White Coyote)

Colquitt, Georgia

Some months after we'd done the Covet *story in* The Gospel Truth, *the woman who told the story came to me with a second story.*

"There is a coyote coming around me."

There are coyotes in that part of Georgia. You hear them sometimes, a pack of them yipping at a distance in the night, and you see their work. You don't leave a puppy or a kitten or even a full-grown dog outside at night without a cage or something substantial to protect it. Creatures as large as new calves are sometimes killed and eaten by coyotes, but you almost never see them, and never during daylight.

"There is a pack of them, and almost every day I drive up at my house after work, by myself, it's broad daylight and nobody's home yet, and the pack will be sitting off in the field next to the house, in the open where I can see them, and a single coyote, a white one, is waiting at the house."

Coyotes aren't usually white.

"I get out of my car, and he follows me like he wants to lick my hand or something. I was afraid at first, but I'm not afraid now. I look at him and he looks back at me, and then I go in and he sits at the door for a while, and then he goes back to the pack, and they leave. He waits for me. He's not here for anybody else, and he's not here if somebody else comes home with me. He's been coming for three or four months. What do you think I should do?"

Why are you asking me?

"He's been coming since you wrote that story."

Oh. Oh, like a revelation. Oh. And sometimes you find something you didn't know you had, and you say the right thing.
    All I know to do is ask the coyote what it wants.

"I can try."

Later, by some months, I saw her again.

"I have the rest of the coyote story."

Paul Harvey has the rest of any number of stories every day on the radio, you just have to listen to the advertisements to get to the rest of the story. With this woman, you get the rest of the story for listening like a human being should, and being at least partially open to the idea that there is more to this world than what you can see with your eyes.

"I woke up from being asleep, in my bed, it was still night. I know I woke up, I know I was awake, I woke up because something was licking my hand. My hand was wet. I woke up to wipe it off. I was wiping it off on the sheet and I started wondering how it got so wet, and I looked beside my bed and there was the coyote. I looked at him and I did what you said. I asked it what it wanted. And the coyote changed. It was the man who sat in that shack and gave me the quarters, and he said, 'I need to be forgiven.' I just looked at him. Forgive him? And then I said, 'I think I can. I don't have to, but I think I can.' And then he was gone. I have not seen the white coyote again since."

———

Thanks, C, especially for your courage . . .

This is the second story in this book written out of my own experience. It is an important story. The White Coyote *story was not used on stage, the story came to me months after we'd already done the* Covet *story in a play called* The Gospel Truth, *and closed that show. I include it on those occasions when I use the* Covet *story in my performances, but I don't use either of them much because it is hard to suggest that I've suddenly morphed into five women on stage. The story is significant because it speaks so directly to what can happen when people tell those stories that truly matter to them. Dr. Elisabeth Kübler-Ross defined the stages of grief and the processes we go through in accepting it. We are still working on how to accomplish recovery from great wrong. Naming and forgiving are known to be important parts. There is a tremendous amount written about "radical forgiveness," the idea that forgiveness is most valuable for the forgiver, not the forgiven, and that forgiveness is the most crucial part of any recovery.* Covet *is about the naming of a huge wrong.* White Coyote *is about coming to forgiveness. The story is not complete without both parts. Now, I can imagine that if this woman had told this* White Coyote *story to a psychiatrist, she might have been put on an anti-hallucinogen, and who knows what else, so that her touch with reality would be appropriately reestablished. But I'm Mama Spider's apprentice. (I wrote a book about being Mama Spider's apprentice,* Spider Speculations, *and I told some of this story in that book.) And it would be hard to imagine a more appropriate or more useful reframing and resolution than the one this woman found for herself.*

Bombs Upstairs

Newport News, Virginia

A WOMAN: When the military took over Mulberry Island and started using it for bombing practice, they told us to put buckets of wet sand around the house, so if we got bombed accidentally we could do something about it.

This was more real than you might think. They were bombing Mulberry Island daily. We were right across the river. And bombs by mistake fell in the water sometimes.

So my mother put buckets of sand around. Five-gallon buckets of sand.

One upstairs, one downstairs.

I have no earthly idea what good a five-gallon bucket of sand would do, but, then, I knew exactly what *I* would do. Say a bomb came through my bedroom ceiling, I'd grab the bomb and stick it in the bucket of sand.

Had to happen fast, of course. So I practiced.

I'd lay in my bed and "notice" something on the floor and leap up, grab the item, and run with it to the bucket of sand and bury it. I did this. I did it seriously.

None of my brothers or sisters practiced the way I did, and I worried about that, but I couldn't make them practice, so I took their responsibility, too.

I'd run into their rooms, grab something from the floor and head back to the bucket of sand. My older sisters did not appreciate this, not in the least. I was an invasion of privacy and given to picking up whatever came to hand which was sometimes rather personal in nature.

My parents didn't stop me. They understood it was what I could contribute to the effort to keep us all safe, and that it was important to my well-being to let me do it.

Now, I'd really like to know whose fine idea it was to tell us to put buckets of sand around in our house. What earthly good is a bucket of sand for a bomb? And why did we do it? How did anyone expect to be any safer for a bucket of sand?

Porchman/Parchman

Port Gibson, Mississippi

Part One

PORCHMAN: The deal rocked up and I killed this man, shot him.
He put it out he was gon' shoot me, he's lookin' for me . . .
said, "If you go home, I'm a kill you; if you stay away, I'm
a kill you."

And I went to a lady's house, friend of mine, and I say,
"Let me borrow your gun, I'm gon' up to Vicksburg, shoot
me some ducks. I'll bring you a couple back." And she say,
"I don't like the look in your eyes." And she won' loan me
no gun, so I go down to Fair Street and I buy one, a shotgun, never been shot before, and twelve shells, no. 4, and
I come out of the store, and the police just standing there,
and I think, Take me now, take me before I do something.
But they talking and laughing, ain't even looked at me.

And I'm gon' home. I figure don' matter what he say, you
can go home when you can't go nowhere else. Except I'm just
comin' down the hill and there he is. He got a friend with
him. I just keep walking, I got my gun under my shoulder
away from him, he don' see it, and I just keep walkin'.

He said, "You gon' be hollerin' in a minute."

I said, "Go on, let me alone." Said, "I'm goin' home, I ain't bothered ya'll."

He said, "I told you I'm gon' put you in hell in time to still get supper."

And when he done this here *(Reaches like he might be getting a gun from his belt)*, I popped him. The deal rocked up. I blowed off his face.

And then, I just walked right by my house, my old lady in there gettin' supper, she ain't knowed nothin', and it's better if she don't. Folks started hollerin' and screamin' up by the road, and I walk on down to the railroad tracks. And I walk that track till 'bout near daylight with that shotgun loaded, and then I decide not to carry the gun no more, and I put it down underneath a bridge. And then, I met two other fellows and we jump a train. Going towards Yazoo City, 'cept we got off before we got there.

And then here come the man, and they say my name and they say I killed a man, and first I say I'm somebody else, but they think I'm one of the other fellows, so I say who I am. See, I ain't just murdered somebody, I killed that man in self-defense. And my name gon' be better if I face it than if I run away. I say who I am, and one of the fellows I'm with, he gets so scared, he have a buck ague. That means he can't hold nothin'. That mean he mess his pants.

So I go to trial, and the man I kill, his boss was a white man and he come into court, and he talk about what a good man this fellow was and how hard-workin' he was, and how he never done nothin' wrong. And it ain' like he was friends with this man, he just know him at work.

And it don't matter that I say he was carrying a gun and he'd been puttin' it out he was gon' kill me, and he stood there in the street and told me he was sending me to hell, none of that don't matter or don't seem to.

The deal rocked up. That white man say I ought to be hanged. And they sentence me to life in prison. And some says that's lucky, but it don't feel so lucky, not for shootin' a man trying to shoot me.

And I go to the penitentiary. Parchman.

I ain' gon' talk much here. I been so crazy I thought the flies was pets, and so hungry I eat clover like a mule. I worked. I hoed more miles than most men ever walked, and in winter we clear more land so next summer we can hoe it too.

I seen men whipped till they bled to death, And I thought maybe I ought to do somethin' get me whipped like that. I seen the miles of graves. Them folks ain't in Parchman anymore.

And one day, this new sergeant come in, and his last name is the same as mine, and he begins to look out for me a little. And about that time, they're asking prisoners to sign up for the army and go to war, and I sign up, but I'm never called, and it turns out almost all the prisoners from Parchman died at Pearl Harbor, and I wasn't one of them, and it was this sergeant kept me out, kept me working my Cadillac hoe in Mississippi. I didn't know whether to thank him or cuss him. He say, "I can't let you go, you running the camp up here."

But he the one recommend me for parole. Thirteen years. And I got out. I was a rattlesnake for a while after I got out. A riled-up rattlesnake.

But I didn't kill nobody else. And now, I couldn't do it, I'd rather die myself.

Now I got arthritis so bad, about all I rattle around is stories. I tell you some stories. Ever' one of them the truth. If I'm lying, I'm dying. My own stories. Other people's stories. I sit here—I'm the Porchman now, that's where you go when you get old—and nobody can tell me something I'm afraid of, I seen about as bad as you can get already. Nobody can tell me something I judge them for, I done too much myself.

But nobody can tell me a story I ain't interested in either. Lord made some strange creatures when he made the two-leggeds, and I'm using my old age to study up on them.

PART TWO

SISTER: Porchman!

PORCHMAN: Yo, Sister.

SISTER: I got you some vegetables here, I seen your garden ain't come in yet . . .

PORCHMAN: I be grateful for that, I was late getting mine in. It will come, but you're right, it ain't here yet. Old Authur Itis, he held me in the bed for a while this spring.

SISTER: It's just the early stuff, some greens and peas and green onions.

PORCHMAN: Sister, I don't mean no insult, but you pull them onions out of that bag and you carry them back home with you . . .

SISTER: Why on earth, you don't like onions?

PORCHMAN: I can't stand the sight of 'em, can't bear to think about the taste.

SISTER: There's nothing better than these little green onions . . .

PORCHMAN: You know where I been in my life?

SISTER: Of course I do, I know that's why you got the arthritis so bad . . .

PORCHMAN: Well, once, about the time I was thinking that whipping might be a way to die and get out, we was out in this huge onion field with them Cadillac hoes, one row at a time for weeks on end, sun up to sun down, and we were hungry, every one of us hungry, and the overseer, he knows we're hungry, and he come up to me and he say, "You see that onion?" He points to where my hoe is working. "That's my onion. You see that grass over there?" And he points to the edge of the field a hundred yards away. "That's yours, you want something to eat, you go eat that grass like the mules do." And what I done, I pulled an onion out of the ground and I stood there in front of him and I ate it. All of it. I ate the roots with the dirt on 'em, I ate the leaves, I ate the onion.

SISTER: What happened?

(A long pause. He won't tell her.)

PORCHMAN: I lost my taste for onion. I be grateful, and I thank you for the greens and the peas, but you take them things back home with you.

SISTER: Whatever. *(Exits)*

David Crosby collected the oral history for this story. David and Patty Crosby and the Mississippi Cultural Crossroads project at Port Gibson, Mississippi, have done some of the best oral history/story-collecting I've had the honor to use. They have published some of their work in a "little" magazine called I Ain't Lying.

Women and Mice

Mouse Stole

East Tennessee

AN OLDER WOMAN: I had a doll, a fancy china doll.

The baby dolls I had were rag, and Mama made them. I was ten, eleven, somewhere in there, about ready to give up dolls, except for this one. It was not a baby doll, it was older. Not like Barbie now, my mother wouldn't have let me have a Barbie. Sometimes I see a doll that is somehow sort of ageless, especially the way people dress them, like the collector dolls, and it makes me remember the one I had.

I made her clothes. I had a collection of fabric scraps Mother gave me, and I could and did spend days making clothes for this doll. Her name was Elizabeth.

Well, I also had the Sears and Roebuck wish book—my mother called it the wish book—and I would go through that looking for the sort of clothes I wanted to create for Elizabeth, and fur (sort of collar-stole things) came into fashion. I mean, it would be fox, or rabbit made to look like fox, and the little fox head would still be on it and would be biting the tail of the next fox, and women wore two or three of these things at a time.

A woman in our church had a set of them, and I thought they were just about the most wonderful thing I'd ever seen, and I determined Elizabeth needed something like that, and the only thing I could think of that might be the right size for Elizabeth was mice.

I needed some mouse fur.

There was none listed in the Sears and Roebuck, but there were plenty in the barn, and all I had to do was get some of them.

I wanted their heads whole, which meant I couldn't use a mousetrap—too many heads got squashed with traps, so I sat in the barn with a trap I made. I had a wooden cigar box, the top of it was open and propped up with a little stick, and I sat about twenty feet away with a string on the stick, and when a mouse went in the box to get the bait, I could pull that string and the lid would fall—and I had a live mouse—and then I could dump the whole box, mouse and all, in a bucket of water and drown the mouse, and have its head whole.

I made Elizabeth sit with me in the barn, and it took two days and a series of refinements on the trap and the choice of bait to get the first mouse, but we did it.

Now, I had seen my father tan hides, I knew what the job was, and it was not the most pleasant thing I've ever done, but I cut the hide off that mouse, preserved the head, treated it with the boric acid and salt, and did it two more times for two more mice. Most of the time when my father did it, he wanted the leather, not the fur, so the fur suffered some, but Elizabeth didn't seem to notice, and I was so proud of myself, I didn't notice either.

Now, it was fall when I did this, and Elizabeth wore that mouse stole for special occasions all winter long, and nobody in her social circle mentioned that her stole still smelled a little, so I didn't either.

But when spring came, I needed to store the stole. That's what the woman at church said she did: "Put it in the cedar chest with her good pillowcases." Well, I put

Elizabeth's mouse stole in the drawer with Mama's good pillowcases, and that was a mistake. They might have been all right if I hadn't tried to leave the heads on the mice, but I did, and I wrapped those mouse skins up very carefully in the best pillowcases because Mama didn't use them.

Mama found Elizabeth's stole by the stink of it, and after she got through hollering, she wanted to know what in the devil this was, and wasn't the least bit sympathetic when I told her.

The pillowcases were ruined, my hide got a better job of tanning than I did on those mice, and—this was what made me really unhappy—Mama threw Elizabeth's stole out in the trash, and I was forbidden to hunt for more mice.

Eden Mouse

Southeast Georgia

*A Storyteller, later joined by Walker, who is, for this scene, a choir-
master, and the Choir he is master of.*

STORYTELLER: I remember family dinners when I was a child,
there'd be so many people—the big table at Grandma's
could seat fifteen or twenty, but it wasn't big enough to seat
everybody, so we'd eat in stages. First seating would be the
men. We children would hang around for that one, we'd be
under everybody's feet, the men were the storytellers, or
I thought so when I was a child. I think now they were the
performers, dinner conversation for them was a friendly
rivalry to see who could make the others laugh. We children liked that, we'd hang around in the doorways and listen, and they knew they had us as audience, too. If there
was a racy story—funny what was racy at the time—we'd
be told to scoot. We'd scoot to where we weren't seen and
continue to try to listen, and even if we couldn't hear the
story, we'd listen for the laughter we knew was coming.

Second seating was us, and it was fast and furious
because after we ate, we went outside to play. The men
would be off somewhere smoking, usually the front porch,

or, if it was too cold, the good parlor, and when the women finally sat to eat, it was just them in that part of the house, and they lingered at the table and talked.

I didn't know, till I was old enough to be part of that group, what went on. They were not performers but they were storytellers. I had an uncle who was late for one of these dinners once and ate with the women that day instead of with the men, and after that, he'd want to wait and eat with the women. If they'd let him, they didn't always.

"Herbert, if you want dinner this year, you need to get here in time to eat with the men. We've got some things to talk about."

I know why he wanted to be there and why they wouldn't let him, it was the stories they told. It was a chance they had to be together and take care of one another. They wouldn't have called what they told stories. They were talking about the events of their lives in the close and private way women can have, particularly women of that generation.

One dinner I remember, I was a child, I ate enough for the next three days at the second seating, and then the whole gaggle of us children, all stuffed, rolled out to the hay barn to play. That day in the barn, in a corner, I found a tiny perfect mouse. It was dead, but it didn't stink, it had died high and dry, so it was preserved, and somehow in my six- or seven-year-old brain, it was beautiful. I picked it up and put it in my pocket.

I eventually wandered back into the house where the women were still sitting at the table. An aunt, a woman who was a nurse and a widow, had come in in the meantime. I was crazy about her and I climbed onto her lap, she holding onto me with her left arm, and finishing her pie and coffee with the right. The collar of her suit had some fur on it, and I was running my hands through it when I remembered the mouse in my pocket, and produced it.

It was my intent to give it to her, I thought it might go with the collar on her suit, but that was not what happened: every woman at that table, my mother among them, rose to her feet, my mouse was immediately done away with. The image I have is like a flock of birds that is mightily disturbed and then, finally, comes to roost again.

I was furious, I thought the mouse was beautiful and I wanted it back, I would take it to my father instead. I would keep it myself. I would take it to school and show my teacher. Somebody besides me would see its value, what was wrong with them?

(Walker leads the Choir in very quietly behind the Storyteller.)

My gracious aunt held me close and explained that one reason people were upset was germs, that dead things were often not very clean, but another reason, and maybe the bigger reason, was that people were uncomfortable with seeing things that were once alive and now dead, and that as I got older, I might get to be uncomfortable with that, too.

(Walker cues the Choir, then, as background music, they begin.)

What my aunt told me was my own personal version of the Garden of Eden story, not that I understood it then. What she told me was that innocence is lost, but one of the things that comes in its place is the knowledge of things like life and death, and that the "fall" would happen to me, too. It did, I do not feel the same way about that mouse, and I wonder now what ever possessed me to think it beautiful.

I also know now what the women in my family did in the long afternoons they lingered over the dinner table, I grew up to be one of them.

Those dinner days were tremendous amounts of work, huge investments in food and labor and time by people who were not rich. All the women pitched in so the work didn't sit so heavy on one or two, but by the time it came their turn to eat, they had prepared and cooked the meal and fed thirty or more people already, washed and dried the dishes they ate off of twice already, and they'd have to do it another time and divide up leftovers before the day was finally done. It was worth it. The stories that passed between them at the third seating were secrets shared, stories that can only come after innocence is lost—they make no sense before.

(Cued by Walker, the Choir comes to a hold, a silence.)

And I know now that innocence has to be lost to be human.

(The Choir, again cued by Walker, completes their song at full voice.)

WALKER *(To the Storyteller, the Choir and the audience at the end of the Choir's song)*: Thank you, thank you . . .

STORYTELLER: Thank you. I didn't know you were bringing in music.

WALKER: Well, I'm trying to please Miss Mary. She wants this like the movies, and the movies always have music at the "fall from innocence" part.

STORYTELLER: Walker, you are a funny man.

WALKER: I take that as a compliment.

Thousands

Chota, Montana

I was visiting in Montana in the dead of winter. It was work or I would have chosen another time of the year. Fifty miles south of the Canadian border, fifty miles east of the front range of the Rockies, and fifty degrees below zero with the windchill.

The windshields of cars cracked in that kind of cold. And even a gasoline engine needed warming before it would start. So you drove up to a telephone pole sort of arrangement, caught an electric cord that was whipping in the wind and plugged up an engine block heater.

Back east in Tennessee, I'd done this for an old diesel engine in the winter there, but I didn't know you could even need to do it for a gasoline engine, too.

"Just if you want the car to start."

Fine. So the morning of the mice, we were out early, and I went straight to the car to get in it and out of the wind.

"You don't want to do that."

My friend unplugged his car from the power pole, opened his door, opened my door, reached in without getting in, and started the engine. And mice, mice by the thousands . . .

"Not thousands."

Mice by the hundreds . . .

"Probably not even hundreds."

What? Mice by the tens? Mice, a lot of mice, started pouring out of the car.

"It is warm—well, relatively warm—when you plug up the block heater and these guys need warm like everything else. They hang out in the engine and come through the firewall when I start it. Can't keep a fire wall in a car here any better than you can keep a windshield. Cold gets the windshield, mice get the fire wall."

Then he put the dogs in the car, they chased out more mice. And then he said:

"Get in."

He *was* a man of few words. So I did get in, and shut the car door, out of the fifty below windchill. Not warm exactly but not as cold as standing outside. He got in, shut his door, and we started rolling. And about two hundred yards down the road, a major question arose in my imagination: what do you do if they are not all out?

"What?"

The mice.

"Oh, I expect you'll do the same thing I do."

And what's that?

"Hold your pant's legs shut."

Hold your pant's legs shut. Not stop the car and try to get the mouse out. Not panic because there is a wild animal loose in the automobile with you. Drive a hundred miles—it was hard not to drive a hundred miles to get anywhere in that incredible place—with your trouser legs held shut.

"Dogs do a pretty good job of getting them out."

I saw no extra mice in the car that morning. But I've thought a lot since about the accommodation made for mice that want as badly as anything else to be warm, and how doing one thing— plugging the car you need up to a block heater so it will start— guarantees a new relationship with something else. In this case, a lot of mice. Thousands of them.

This man had met me at the airport looking a lot like something out of a cartoon: he was covered with grease, he had spent the day rebuilding the engine in an old harvester, a machine almost the size of my little house, instead of trying to buy a new one, and the first thing he said when I met him was:

"You know Wendell Berry?"

I've read him.

"SOB ruined my life."

Not exactly. But the endeavor of sustainability made high, dry-land wheat farming a lot more complicated. And made this man a diesel mechanic along with everything else.

Somewhere down the Rube Goldberg construction that becomes a life, any life, that particular one included the accommodation of a lot of mice. So you learn to hold your pant's legs shut. It is doable.

Thanks, Ralph P. This is the third of the stories in this book that is written out of my experience.

Mules

Amish Mule

Lancaster, Pennsylvania

A DOCTOR: I am from here and this is a snow and a mule story. My wife and I needed to soak up some sunshine and we'd been to Bermuda on vacation.

We'd heard there was a snowstorm in the Northeast, but we didn't realize how bad the storm was. We tried to land in New York and couldn't. We landed in Norfolk, Virginia, and it was the next day before we could get into New York. And when we climbed on the train about one in the morning, we felt we were finally on our way home to Lancaster.

Except the train ground to a stop every few minutes because the snow clogged the filters on the engine, and somebody had to go clean it out, so it was another twenty-four hours getting to Lancaster. And we still needed to get home.

We called Ann's mother—she had the children—and she said don't even try it yet, there were drifts of snow to the top of the telephone poles, twenty or more feet deep, and we couldn't get in the door if we did get there. We were exhausted. We were at a restaurant that belonged to a friend of ours, and he offered that we should stay with him and his wife until the roads were passable. We were grateful, we took him up on the offer.

We called Ann's mother back to say what we were doing, and I crawled into bed. Hadn't been there five minutes, Ann's mother called back. A patient of mine was starting labor at home about six miles down the road from where I was. She couldn't get to the hospital. Could I get there? Now, labor is a natural process that comes to a natural end, and most of the time, you are best leaving nature and the mother to do the work, but this woman was older, mid-forties, and while she had had other children, so late a child is a cause for some concern for the well-being of the mother and the child.

I said I'd try to get there.

My friend loaned me warm clothes, we made up what we could of a doctor bag, and he went back over to the restaurant and asked his customers, could anybody get six miles down the road? There was an Amish man, said he had a horse that could do it, and thirty minutes later, he was back at the restaurant sitting in the saddle of one horse and leading a second.

Now, I'd ridden a horse in my younger years and this six miles would have been a real pleasure but for the snow. Man handed me the second horse and turned his around and went back home.

I got on her, and we set out. This was hard going. She was a good mare, but half the time she was trying to walk chest deep in snow, and after about three miles she was worn out. I tried breaking path for her, but after a hundred feet, I was as worn out as she was. It became evident to me that the mare was not going to be able to go another three miles in unbroken snow.

Well, I knew of another Amish fellow lived close there. I can't say he was a friend exactly, I didn't know him very well, but I knew of him. That mare and I barely made it to his barn, friend or not. The horse would have broken her heart trying for me, she was good, but it was just too hard.

I told this fellow what my problem was, and he hauled out this old red mule, huge animal, put the exhausted horse in the mule's stall, put the saddle on the mule and said, "She'll get you there."

And get me there, she did. We spent an hour or more digging out of a drift she keeled over sideways into. Wasn't her fault, you couldn't see what was solid and what wasn't. And I was grateful for that mule, because she wasn't about to stay stuck in anything any longer than she had to, and we got out. I put my bag, such as it was, back together and climbed back on her.

She was ready to go home right then, but after some discussion, she agreed we might go on. And something like nine hours after I got the phone call for help, I got to the woman's house in time to deliver a baby girl she and nature would have done just fine with.

Next morning, I rode the mule back to where she came from, told the man thanks, picked up the horse, rode her back to where she came from. It was much easier going back because tracks were broken.

And then I slept for a very long time. There's a snowstorm story for you. And a big red mule story, too. I can't say she was a particularly comfortable ride or much of a sight to look at under saddle, but I came to genuinely admire that mule in the time I spent in her company.

Three Mule Stories

Colquitt, Georgia

Mule One

A MAN: I remember when my daddy traded his mules for a tractor. He had to have the tractor, had to find some way to get more acres in crops, and a tractor could do that, but he had raised and trained those mules, and they were good and he loved them, and I swear they loved him. You had to have the cash down payment for a tractor or a trade-in, and those boys that sold the equipment weren't dummies, and they knew if they took a man's mules as a trade-in, then he was going to have to come back to them for parts and service on his tractor, so they took mules. Sold them for slaughter, so they didn't make near what they gave on them, but they knew it was good business in the long run. Well, the day they delivered my dad's first tractor, he pointed them over to where the mules were standing and said, "There's your mules," and he set out walking back across the farm. He stayed gone all day. He couldn't watch, he knew what was going to happen to those mules and he hated it, but he didn't see he had any other choice.

Mule Two

A MAN: Working mules is an art. A mule cares about his kind more than he cares about your kind, so he is more inclined to listen to the fellow hitched up next to him than he is to a human being. What you have to do is convince him that you are another mule and that you are bigger and smarter than he is. One way to do that is to get him when he is young and still small enough you can pick him up and carry him around a little and to do that very thing. Rest of his life, he'll remember that, and think you can still lift him off of his four feet and tote him around. So he listens to you 'cause he don't want to be lifted off of his four feet. He's a flight animal, running away is his best defense, and he can't run away without his feet on the ground. This is also true for a horse. When a mule turns around to face you on his own, with his ears pricked up and paying attention, you are the next mule up in the pecking order and that's exactly what you want to be. You do not ever want to try to beat a mule into obedience. You can beat a mule into a sort of submission but you make a real enemy that way, an enemy with a memory like an elephant who will wait until an opportune moment and try to kill you. You work a mule by showing him his life is easier and more interesting if he is doing what you want. He is not afraid to work, truth is he likes your attention, and he's actually pretty willing if you can tell him in mule what you want him to do. Next trick is learning to talk mule. It is almost all gesture and attitude. Now, you can punish a mule if it is just punishment. He'll accept justice and respect you for it. He'll even test you and expect justice. But it is a fool beats a mule just because he is pissed. Same goes for dogs and children.

Mule Three

A WOMAN: My grandmother had no education beyond grade eight, but she married a man with a little more, he was her schoolteacher when they eloped, and she set out to leave the land. She'd had all she was going to take of a brutal father and scratching in dirt. She pushed Granddaddy into lots of things he wasn't very good at—insurance salesman, furniture salesman—and their life was not easy. They made it through the Depression with him selling household stuff door to door and her taking in sewing, but she had had all she was going to eat of souse meat and she did not regret leaving the farm. Her sister's husband still farmed, and he had an old team of mules that had never been noted for their willingness or cooperation: John and Henry. The only joke I ever heard the woman make or tell was about her brother-in-law and those two mules. She named her own feet John and Henry, and if there was something that was going to be hard, or she didn't especially want to do it, she'd start talking to her feet like her brother-in-law had to talk to those mules: "GET UP, JOHN! HUP, HENRY, HUP! MOVE IT, YOU SONS OF DONKEYS! HUP!" She could sound exactly like her brother-in-law. She'd climb the stairs at the end of the day, yelling at her feet: "HUP, MULES, HUP!" Now, it was funny, but she didn't do it just for the laughs. Granddaddy told the jokes and stories, not her. And you had to have heard the man to know she was imitating him. She didn't tell you. For a long time, I thought she was just making fun, but I don't think so anymore. She did it because it reminded her of how far she'd come and that, even if she was dog tired, whatever it was she had to do wasn't as hard as plowing with those two mules.

The first mule story is Billy Kimbrel's story. He's speaking about his father. The second is a briefing of good training techniques. The third story is actually from my grandmother. I wrote it for Colquitt because I needed a third story that somehow spoke of mules, but after we did it, a woman who saw the show said her mother did the same thing, especially going upstairs. Her mother's mules were Bess and Anna. I have since learned of other situations in which people called their feet their mules and named them. Seems, at one time, it wasn't all that uncommon a joke to make. It is—obviously—a joke that no longer has much meaning because nobody has to work a team of mules for a living anymore, so nobody knows what work that is. But I do love finding such little gems of heritage such as this one.

Characters

Secret Marriage

Colquitt, Georgia

A YOUNG WOMAN: I married March the nineteen, and I was seventeen going on thirty-five.

Now, my mother had married a man she just knew six weeks, and turned over her fiancé to do it, and then called her husband "Mister" for the rest of her forty years of marriage to him. I asked her why and she said she just knew him six weeks which was not long enough to be on a first-name basis.

So I had that and I was quite a young sophisticate myself, and I went with older people, as witness the fact I married somebody six years older than I was. I already knew more than my parents, I knew more than anybody except my grandmother. I do bow to her knowledge.

And I visited Grandmother during the summer. And there wasn't anything to do here but flirt.

Now, I had one boyfriend. Well, I had lots of "boy friends," but one boyfriend who wanted to marry me, Julian, and he was going to be a minister, but he didn't live here.

And Zack did.

And I was here during the summers. Everybody met at the drugstore in the afternoons and had a coca cola—there wasn't anything else to do—and most everybody had ice cream with their coca cola

But I had a dill pickle and crackers with mine.

And Zack would ride up on that big black horse. He knew where we were, and what we were doing, and we'd gotten all dressed up . . . And Zack had a crush on me.

All the boys did.

Now, I loved to dance. You couldn't dance in Colquitt. It wasn't religion, it was just country. There wasn't anywhere to dance, but I was from Americus, and there was the Windsor hotel. I've danced a million miles in the Windsor hotel. I learned to dance in Montezuma. Everybody danced in Montezuma.

In Americus, I danced with the boy who was going to be a minister that I was supposed to marry, Julian, and I danced with the pitcher of the baseball team, the best-looking man I've ever seen: snapping eyes, wavy dark hair and beautiful teeth.

He would have married me, too, but I didn't see the future in baseball.

And Zack didn't ride that big horse to Americus; he didn't dance. You couldn't teach Zack anything. He was a lawyer. His daddy was, too, but they didn't practice together. Couldn't get along.

Grandma would let Zack come around to see me, but just for certain hours, and we had to sit on the porch in the evening.

When I was home, Zack wrote to me and told me that, as an older person, he thought it was his duty to tell me I was wasting my time with a ballplayer and a minister. When I was here, the minister wrote to tell me I was wasting my time with a lawyer because it was an amoral profession, and a ballplayer who wouldn't amount to anything anyway.

The ballplayer never wrote. Maybe that's why I didn't marry him.

And Zack had this friend, Hunter, who lived in the same town I did, and he told Hunter to keep an eye out on me, and Hunter took that to mean keep me busy.

And Hunter had this horse, you could just lean and it would go that direction and jump logs and, well, anything.

So Hunter and I rode horses and he fell in love with me. He was besotted. It was a soap opera. And that fancy horse was my horse when we rode. I loved him.

And I wrote Zack and Julian and the ballplayer all Dear John letters, I told them I was in love with Hunter, and Zack wouldn't have it. He told Hunter he better back off, that I was probably just in love with that horse.

And Hunter did it.

Now, I was young and fickle and I did love that horse, but if Hunter had had a backbone of his own, I might have married him. And I went to Grandma's in Colquitt to recover my heart.

And, of course, Zack was there.

First thing he did was tell me I was only in love with a horse, and that I'd get over it. And I said to hell with that, that I was going home. I didn't use profanity then, but I do now. Get as old as I am, you get to use it. Then, I started trying to call my daddy, but I had to go by Zack's office to use the phone because Grandma didn't have a phone.

We had phones in Americus. We had indoor plumbing in Americus.

Well, Zack would see me go by, and the operator would interrupt me when I was just starting to call, and say Zack's on the phone, he says it's important that he speak to you.

I'd say, "What are you calling me for, I'm not talking to you."

And he'd say, "Wait another day, I've got something I want to tell you."

"'Wait,' my foot! You're the man thinks I'm in love with a horse."

And this happened three or four times, and he saw I was determined to go home, and he came up with this idea of a secret marriage. He was a lawyer, he could talk you into anything.

He'd already asked me to marry him and I'd said maybe, but I'd said maybe to Julian, too, and he knew it, and I'd written them all Dear John letters, but I liked the idea of a secret marriage.

A secret marriage in a secret place. Near Laurel Bush Springs.

Zack got a shave at the barbershop every other day and he didn't even get an extra one for the secret wedding because he was afraid somebody would be suspicious, which was ridiculous. The barber wouldn't have thought anything. And Grandma took a nap in the afternoon, and that's when I got out. They all ate so much for dinner they'd just pile in the bed afterwards and go to sleep. A friend of Zack's picked me up in a car.

Well, Zack was all bib and tucker, except he needed a shave, and I was dressed, let me tell you. Brown, brown satin with a bustle. Some people can wear black, but brown's my color, goes with red hair. The very best brown kid shoes. A hat with a veil.

Zack got himself and the preacher and another witness and we were married.

I was seventeen going on thirty-five.

And we came back into town in separate cars so nobody would know. And the next day I got on the train to go home, and Zack was there, and he kissed me good-bye.

I said, "You shouldn't do that, what if somebody sees you."

And he says, "Well, I can kiss my wife, can't I?"

And I said, "I'm none your wife yet."

He got off the train, and I went on to Americus, and I tell you, I meant to have me a trousseau, and I had the dressmaker going, and I had Pinkston's going, and I told my father I was getting married.

Of course, I was already married but I was scared to tell him that.

I told Zack two months because that was how long I thought it would take me to get my trousseau together.

But Zack called in a week and said he was coming to get me.

He'd let the cat out of the bag. He had to come. He was listening to Emma Mae play sentimental music on the piano and he just up and said, "I have to go get my wife."

And Papa, well, he was indulgent with me, he loaned us his car to drive my trousseau back to Colquitt.

And that's how I got married.

I taught expression for shy children till I got pregnant with my first child. He stayed in the pelvis too long and he came out with an egg-shaped head, fiery red, and wrinkled up. Nicest thing anybody could say was that he looked like he'd make a fine lawyer, and he did.

———

Thanks, Juanita Geer.

The Patternmaker

Lima, Ohio

The Patternmaker speaks to the audience, but he speaks as if someone in the audience is a new apprentice. He will need, over the course of three appearances, some tools of his own for measuring, for instance, calipers—a tape measure won't cut it. He will need a truly beautiful wooden gear that comes in on a pulley of some sort. Make it at least eighteen inches in diameter, but larger is better (steam engines for trains were very big). And he will need a set of technical drawings (blueprints) for machinery pieces.

Part One

THE PATTERNMAKER: I cannot pretend to speak of the measure of a man or the pattern of a place, but a machine is different. You can measure a machine and imagine its parts, you can create and assemble a machine.

This morning, we need a gear. Not just any gear, we need a gear that fits and functions, a gear that has a place and a job in the transfer of power in a machine.

It has a specific size: a radius, a diameter, and a relationship between the two: 3.14159, and so forth, never ending, never repeating, a magical number called pi. Pi is important in this work. But a gear is three-dimensional so it is, mathematically, a cylinder. Some gears are cones. Some are molded as parts of drive shafts or crank shafts or wheels, cylinders on cylinders, cones on cylinders, cylinders on polyhedrons, but not yet, those are harder.

This morning we need a simple gear for a complex machine.

When I was an apprentice, I swept the shavings from beneath the benches of the masters for years before I was allowed a block of wood to cut. But they say you are advanced and ready for simple gears.

We shall see. Whose son are you?

This gear has thirty-two cogs, which must be spaced and shaped perfectly to mesh with the next gear of a different radius and diameter, which it will drive. This gear has a indentation in it, a small square hole that does not go all the way through it, that is off-center, so a certain volume of a specific dimension in a specific place must be removed. And this gear has a hole through it, also of specific dimensions that must be perfectly round and perfectly centered and must be a perfect ninety degrees through it.

The numbers are here on the drawing. You can read?

And here is a cube of mahogany. The gear you will make is in it, and must be cut out.

When you finish, you will have the pattern from which the missing gear can be molded.

We shall see how you do, Apprentice.

PART TWO

THE PATTERNMAKER: Tools? What do you mean you need to borrow tools? Are you telling me you have no tools?

My God, a horse with no legs, a man with no hands. No tools! Would you talk with no language, sing with no voice?

I have heard it said that a good carpenter could build a house with a three-pound hammer and a sharp pocket-knife, but that is after he has mastered tools, all of them, after he knows their functions, their value and their limits, and how to make other things serve their purpose. Before he understands his tools, he might build a shed or a chicken coop that stands for a year or two, but nothing more substantial.

And a house, well, even the best house is a great slipshod hulk of an affair that hides quarter-inch imperfections in every joist.

A gear in a machine does not tolerate such chasms of imperfection. A machine would shake to pieces. A machine would explode.

A machine needs precision. "Precision." I love the very word.

No tools. So. You must start like the rest of us after all.

You must determine what you need to do the job, and you must make your own tools.

PART THREE

THE PATTERNMAKER: Well, there you are. I do hope you have something to show me. You had better, the century is turning.

(A gear, a beautiful big, wooden gear, comes in on a pulley.)

Yes. The missing gear. It is beautiful. But is it to the proper dimensions?

Function, you know. Function is more important in this work than the aesthetic values of the object. But it would be a cold man who did not see the beauty of it.

I am not so cold myself.

(He prepares to measure the gear.)

This is the test, Apprentice. This tests the gear; it tests the maker of the gear, it also tests the tools you made to make this gear. If the tools are not accurate . . .

(He measures the gear.)

Ah, this is good. This is very good indeed. With this, Apprentice, you have learned the mathematics, and the craft. You have made of yourself a skilled man.

But the century is turning. The century, no, the millennium.

The truth is the machine that needs this gear is obsolete. You did take your time to make it. But let me assure you there is another that wants your skills.

(He pulls out blueprints with each.)

This one is an engine in a truck. This, a jet engine . . .

This one is your future.

It should not take so long again. You own the tools now, you made them; more, you have the knowledge to make any further tools you need, you earned it.

Go. You are valuable. Make yourself useful.

If some object you make happens to be particularly beautiful—aside from its function of course, its function is always first—I would be grateful if you think of me.

Most of the patternmaker's work is now done by computer and machine, so the patternmaker himself is obsolete, but the patternmaker used to be a truly skilled job in a foundry operation. Lima, Ohio, was where the Lima steam engines for trains were made. Made: designed; the parts cast in a foundry; machined to tolerance; and those huge engines assembled from their separate pieces, fired up to make sure they held their steam like they should; then driven away to become part of the making and running of the railroad in this country. A few of the old Lima steam engines were, at the time this piece was written, still in use in China. A patternmaker took a drawing of a part, and made a model of that part from wood; the wood shape he created was used to make a mold, usually a sand mold, and the part was cast from the mold by pouring molten metal into the sand mold. The part was then machined to remove rough edges and fitted into its place in the machine. The wood model served again and again in the making of molds as long as that particular part was in demand. The patternmaker's accurate work was absolutely critical. Couldn't be done without him. The first job of a wannabe patternmaker was to make his own tools. And, of course, his tools had to be accurate for his models to be accurate. What a metaphor.

False Witness

Colquitt, Georgia

THE PREACHER'S WIFE: Most of the time, after a sermon, Jack
would be invited to dinner somewhere with one of the congregation, and you never knew what you were going to get
to eat because people in the church took turns feeding the
preacher, and some of them didn't have so much as others,
and some of them looked at feeding the preacher as an
obligation to be got through and not as something to be
given joyously. I didn't go with him much, I had my children to tend to, and children would have been an extra burden on the family that was feeding him.

Some of these churches were so poor that people never
paid a preacher in money, they'd give him what they called
a "pantry shower" and he'd take his pay home in food.

Well, this once, the children were at his mother's, and
I went with him to Sunday dinner. We got to the house,
and as we were going in, the woman picked up a previously
used cud of tobacco off the front porch rail and put it in her
mouth. And we got inside, and there was a sort of sand pile
around the woodstove, and that was where she spit. There
was an old red dog that came in with us and he laid down
in the sand pile, in the spit—it was warm, you know—and

he rolled over a lot to scratch his back, got up and shook, and laid down again.

That was hard for me.

And she started putting stuff on the woodstove to warm it. It was all cooked already, it just wanted warming. And that dog, well . . . I saw she had some sweet potatoes, and I figured I could eat one of them because they still had the skin on them and I could peel it off and eat the inside, but it turned out they weren't for Sunday dinner, they weren't cooked yet, they were for supper and what was for dinner was chicken and dumplings in what looked like dishwater. She served up the chicken and dumplings in bowls.

I didn't dare look at the bowls or the spoons.

Remember, all the time she has this tobacco in her mouth and she's spitting. And the dog is rolling and shaking. And I know I can't eat this. I can't do it. And the truth is, I don't want Jack to eat it either, but I can't stop him, and he sees it as his duty to partake of what is offered. And I know I'm going to lie to get out of it, and I just hope the Lord doesn't get too mad at me. This is a sort of love offering but maybe it is better to refuse it than it is to throw it up.

So I took a fainting spell. I'd seen them but I'd never had one, and if I say so myself, I took a good one. I had to go outside for air. And then I just couldn't eat a thing, couldn't even drink a glass of milk. I sat in a chair away from the table for dinner while they ate. Jack did his duty and claimed it wasn't as bad as it looked.

Then, going home, he said he knew I faked a fainting spell, and I told him it was the dog that did it.

And he said I was raised picky.

And I said I was raised clean, and didn't intend to change.

And he said most of life is not as clean as you seem to think it ought to be, and you're going to have to get used to it if you eat dinner with me at these country churches.

And I said fine. Fine, fine, fine. And I have not gone with him to another of those Sunday dinners yet.

There are three stories in this collection from the "Swamp Gravy" play The Gospel Truth. *It was the show I needed the sinners for, the one over which I pitched the temper tantrum that named this book. We found some wonderful sinners and some truly terrible ones. We also found a revival preacher, a man who never had a church of his own, a man who traveled the South with a big tent and a specialty sermon on the Ten Commandments. In his sermon, with each commandment, he'd bust a dinner plate over the pulpit to demonstrate what happened to sinners who broke that commandment. He was too good to leave out. We used a lot of second-hand plates producing* The Gospel Truth. *With each of the commandments, I used a story from the oral histories that either kept or broke that commandment.* Covet, *the story of childhood abuse, is one of them: "Thou shall not covet . . ." This is the second story: "Thou shall not bear false witness . . ." The third is* The Postman *story in the last section of this book, "Thou shall have no other gods before me . . ."*

The Butcher Loved Her

Newport News, Virginia

*The graveyard. All the residents are there. Pearl Eby is now there—
she died in the play's first act. Zack Cole approaches her grave.*

PART ONE

GRAVEYARD RESIDENT: Quiet! Someone has some company . . .

(Zack comes to beside Pearl's grave.)

ZACK: Hello. Me—maybe the last man on earth you ever
thought about. I brought you some flowers. Nothing fancy,
just what grows wild on the way here and a couple of Mrs.
Schrack's roses. They were sticking their pretty faces
through the fence. I came to say something but . . .

(He is about to go, but then he looks around and he sits.)

Ah! Nobody is going to hear it, I might as well let my old
heart say what's in it . . . We might have married by now,
you know. Might be talking over dinner instead of over a

mound of dirt. Yes, I'm a little old, and, yes, you were a little young. Yes, you had a young man you were maybe going to marry. I knew all that when you were alive. But you died, and got me instead of him. We could have married, worse has happened in this world. I would have treated you good. Be a young man's slave or an old man's pet. Somebody said that, I don't remember who, but it has the ring of truth to me. If you'd a had me, of course. If your daddy would a let you. I'm not one of you Anabaptists. And the butcher is always suspect: "Think of what he does to all those furry little animals, what would he do to a wife?" My father warned me about that when he taught me the trade. Well, they're happy enough to eat those furry little animals when they are lamb chops, and not lambs anymore. Enough. I make myself too sad when I think about what might have been.

I'll come talk to you again, if you don't mind . . .

(Zack exits.)

GRAVEYARD RESIDENT: Well, that's a revelation.

PART TWO

Zack Cole approaches the grave of Pearl Eby.

ZACK: Me again. I brought you some flowers. What I could find by the side of the road and a couple of Mrs. Burkholder's lilies. I know they don't last long, but they are so pretty while they are there, their faces are so open. You can look down the throat of a lily and see the hand of God. My mother used to say that.

There is some news with me. I've had my coffin built. I wanted one that fit. I've heard of people being tucked into uncomfortable positions to fit in a coffin, and I didn't want that to happen to me. I've been testing it, sleeps good. That's all I needed to know. I don't put the lid on, testing it, I just lay down in it, and sleep. Nobody's going to bring me flowers. That's ok. I don't need them, and I expect Mrs. Burkholder will be glad when somebody quits cutting her lilies.

I've been thinking of joining your church, that way I could be buried in this cemetery. See, I'd like to be buried next to you, if you don't mind, and if I joined the church, I could ask for that . . .

(Two women enter.)

WOMAN 1: Zack Cole! You!

ZACK: Yes, ma'am . . .

WOMAN 2: Are you the person who leaves the flowers for Pearl?

ZACK: I am. It's no secret. I sit here for a while and talk to her sometimes, too.

WOMAN 1: But we didn't know, it has been a mystery here for years, who put flowers on Pearl's grave . . .

ZACK: No mystery.

WOMAN 1: Oh, yes. You didn't know?

ZACK: What's to know?

WOMAN 2: Zack, do you mind if I ask why?

ZACK: Why what?

WOMAN 1: Why Pearl? Why the flowers? She's not your family. Why so long?

ZACK: How long?

WOMAN 2: Twenty years.

ZACK: No.

WOMAN 1: Yes!

ZACK: I didn't know it had been that long.

WOMAN 2: Why, Zack?

ZACK: Well, she was sweet and kind. She'd come into the shop and laugh and talk about things besides another cut of meat, she was kind . . .

WOMAN 2: That's all?

ZACK: Should there be some other reason? Is kindness not enough?

Pearl Eby is buried in the Mennonite cemetery in Newport News. She died when she was eighteen during the flu epidemic of 1918. Not long after, her family left Newport News, so there is no other from her family buried there. Zack Cole, a butcher by trade, did join the Mennonite church late in his life, and is buried next to her because the community honored his request to be put there. He brought fresh flowers to her grave for more than twenty years. It was a mystery in that community for years until somebody found him there.

Exceptional
Experience

Rattlesnake

Walton County, Florida

Jo Carson's continuing search for the perfect barbecue.
   Three Benchwarmers, BW2 and BW3 should be men, BW1 is a woman.

Part One

BW1: I hear you round up rattlesnakes here.

BW2: Used to. Yep. Fun.

BW3: Tons of fun. Tons of snakes, too.

BW1: I see. Round them up and let them go?

BW2: No, no, round them up and eat them.

BW1: Eat them?

BW3: You ever tasted rattlesnake?

BW1: Not that I know of.

BW3: Oh, they're better than squid, better than alligator, better than escargot, they're a genuine delicacy.

BW1: Are they?

BW2: You eat oysters?

BW1: Can't stand the sight of them.

BW2 *(To BW3)*: She may have some trouble with rattlesnake.

BW3: It don't look like oysters, looks like chicken meat except it's round. Looks like chicken filet mignon. Tastes a little like chicken, just earthier. Rattlesnake burger. Nothing like it. Slice of tomato, slice of onion, little bit of mayo, slice of snake.

BW1: Slice of snake.

BW3: Big thick slice of snake.

BW2: Or barbecued. I like my rattlesnake barbecued. Make my own sauce. Mustard sauce. South Carolina mustard sauce.

BW3 (*A loaded question*): Where you from?

BW2: My mama's from South Carolina, she brought the mustard sauce recipe with her when she married a *Florida* boy.

BW1: How do you barbecue a rattlesnake?

BW2: There's two ways. The purest is going to make up his sauce and light his fire before he goes to get his snake, so he has a good bed of coals when he is ready to start. He's gonna cut the head and rattles off the snake, skin it, gut it, pull the backbone out of it, and stick a spit back down the hole the backbone came out of. And he's gonna turn that snake on the spit over the bed of coals, slathering it regular with the sauce, and eat it right off the spit. Good stuff. The other way is to slice the snake, fire up the gas grill and, cook it. Same as chicken. It's good that way, but there's nothing like spit-cooked rattlesnake.

BW3: Now, if you're not the outdoor type, you can do rattlesnake nuggets, that's rattlesnake cut in chunks, battered up with flour and fried in bear grease, but that entails having come onto some bear grease before you get the rattlesnake. I have to watch my cholesterol and that's pretty high cholesterol. Cholesterol's dangerous stuff. So I just grill the rattlesnake.

BW1: Say, theoretically, that I wanted to fix some rattlesnake for supper. I march into the Winn-Dixie and where do I look? Fresh meat?

BW2: Well, never mind the Winn-Dixie. Just go out in the woods . . .

BW1: Go out in the woods?

BW2: . . . and find a snake hole, pour some gasoline down it . . .

BW3: Not gasoline, you knothead. Gasoline ruins the taste of the meat. Ruins it. You ain't from here, you're lying about your *Florida* daddy. Dreaded Northern interloper. Ammonia. You pour ammonia down the snake hole and out comes the snake. Voilà! Supper. How many are you feeding?

BW1: Six.

BW3: Light eaters or heavy eaters?

BW1: Big eaters.

BW3: Need two three-footers or one good five-footer and some vegetables. Say green beans and okra, potato salad and peeled sliced tomatoes.

BW1: Five-foot snake.

BW3: You don't get five feet of snake meat, you've got to cut off the head and the poision gland and the rattles. By the way, don't just leave the head laying around where you're working. It can still bite for a day or two. There are those that will tell you the head is best handled from a distance with a pair of bolt cutters, but I just use regular pliers or barbecue tongs. They do just fine. Bolt cutters are not necessary. An affectation in my opinion. Like the people who wear snake boots and those big metal worker's gloves. Not necessary. Truth is, I do the head and tail out in the backyard with an ax. But here's what you have to remember about doing it outside. You have to hold on to the body of the snake or it can still get away. You look pretty silly chasing a snake with no head down the street. "Catch it, it's supper!

BW1: Fine. Just fine. I don't have to catch chicken. I don't have to kill it. It won't try to bite me. And I don't have to chase it down the street.

BW2: Oh, yeah. One more thing. Be real careful when the snake first comes out of the hole after you've poured the ammonia in on it. It's not real happy then either. Might just ought to wait for the rattlesnake roundup.

Part Two

Same three Benchwarmers.

BW2: In the fifties they did rattlesnake roundups in Freeport, Florida.

BW3: Now that was fun.

BW1: How do you round up rattlesnakes? Saddle up your horse and start singing "Get Along Little Rattlers"?

BW2: No, no. Leave the horse at home. You need a croaker sack, and, according to this fellow, ammonia.

BW3: And a grappling stick.

BW2: Some folks don't need the stick.

BW3: Some folks aren't the brightest.

BW1: And some of those are dead.

BW2: Whoa!

BW1: Now, I sat here and listened to you two tell how to barbecue a rattlesnake and I didn't say anything. You think you're very funny, but I don't think snakes are all that funny. You start on funny snakes again, and I'll tell you about trying to keep a litter of kittens from being a very large, very determined, water moccasin's supper. Happened in my garage. I couldn't stop throwing things at it long enough to get inside and load a gun or it would have gotten the kittens. I wanted the kittens, a full-grown cat helps keep snakes away. Here's the comedy. I finally stopped it when it was coming after me by dropping fifty pounds of potted plant on its head. I couldn't throw fifty pounds, I had to wait till the snake was close enough to me to drop the potted plant. Then we shot it and buried it, and in the morning it was gone from the hole we buried it in.

BW2: Now, those water moccasins . . . Nobody I know is recommending trying to rodeo water moccasins. You can catch rattlesnakes. Rattlesnakes are polite society compared to water moccasins. Rattlesnakes are shy.

BW1: Ok, how about the time I carried sleeping bags inside that I'd been airing out in the yard after a camping trip, and found ground rattlers in them, which were then loose in my den.

BW3: Should have eaten them.

BW1: Did. Fried. In corn oil. In my opinion, the only good snake is a dead snake and I still don't want to see it. The exception to that is black snakes and chicken snakes, they eat poisonous snakes' eggs, but I don't won't to see them either. I'm ready to move to Ireland. They don't have snakes in Ireland. I'm tired of walking out my door with an eye out for snakes. We've got every kind of poisonous snake there is in this country here, and I've seen them all. In my yard.

BW2: Part of what the roundup did was control the population of rattlesnakes.

BW1: So people could move in and cut down more of the forest and build condominiums.

BW3: You don't vote Republican, do you.

BW1: I know two stories from the rattlesnake rodeo that are worth telling. One was a man hitching a ride, and a pickup truck stops to pick him up. There are already three people in the cab and, yes, they are going to Freeport. There is no room in the cab but he is welcome to climb in the back. He does. They start rolling again. They get up to speed. The man in the back begins to notice that the people in the cab keep looking back at him. Then he notices what he is in the back with, a whole bunch of croaker sacks that are tied at the top. And then he starts to notice that the croaker sacks are moving, it is not just the wind moving them. And then he realizes that these folks have been rounding up rattlesnakes for the rodeo contests—biggest snake, most snakes by a single person—they are participants, and he is in the back of the truck with the snakes.

BW2: He lived through it.

BW1: He got out at his first opportunity. When the truck slowed for a car that was turning on the highway, he jumped.

BW3: They were tied up in croaker sacks, he could have ridden on in to Freeport just fine.

JO CARSON

BW1: He chose not to stay in harm's way. Like I said, smart man. In my opinion. Second story: this woman wanted to participate in the rodeo and her husband wanted nothing to do with it, so she went out into the woods herself and found a huge rattler up in a tree. Came back and told her husband. He still wanted nothing to do with it. So she got a neighbor who was willing, they got a ladder, and went back out—the snake was still there—set up the ladder and caught the snake tail first. No ammonia, no grappling stick, no croaker sack. Tail first. And they didn't get bit. She didn't win the contest, she came in second. Somebody else had found a bigger snake.

BW3: That's pretty good.

BW1: It is a story about how God protects fools. Even if He doesn't give them first prize at the Rattlesnake Rodeo. And one more story. I ran over the biggest rattlesnake I've ever seen, I don't know that I killed it, I don't know whether it eventually died of this incident or not, but I did run over it. I was coming from Seagrove, headed to the highway on my way to a Girl Scout honors banquet in an old station wagon known as the "green bomb." I saw the snake, it stretched from one side of the road to the other off both sides, so I didn't see the head or tail, and I thought they'd put in a speed bump. It was that big. I slowed to cross it like I slow to cross speed bumps, slowing down was not an option, the bomb was on its last shock absorbers. Except, of course, it moved when I ran over it. And I saw what it was when it moved. I have witnesses to this, three of my children were also in the car. Now, I told this story at a picnic about a week after it happened, and a man who was listening almost tried to punch me out. My husband stopped him. He was not upset because I might have killed a snake, not at all, he didn't want that snake to be there, he wanted me to say I just made the story up, he wanted his pictures prettier than that. What he knew of the out-of-doors was a golf course and he didn't want something so large and so dangerous to be alive so close to his children. And he was going to punch me because I was the bearer of such news. Sort of a classic "kill the messenger" situation. Now, you go on, tell me how to catch rattlesnakes and be really funny about it. I'm told there is humor in everything if you just learn to see it.

BW 3: Well, did you like the taste of those snakes you ate?

BW 1: Tasty. Very tasty. And no question, I certainly preferred eating them to sleeping with them in the house.

———

Carol McCrite ran over the big snake, dropped the potted plant on the water moccasin and found the ground rattlers in the sleeping bags. Not in the same week. Maybe not in the same year. But, in the same life for sure.

Bass Hammock

Colquitt, Georgia

OLDER MAN: There was a place called Bass Hammock, it was close to a thousand acres of swampland that had never been cleared. It was still like it was when the Indians were here.

There was a big old tree back in there that my grand-daddy had carved his initials in, and he'd showed it to me when he was still alive.

The center of the swampland was a black water with cypress trees and alligators and all kinds of fish. In the spring of the year, you could stand the mosquitoes. It was a magical place with all the spring stuff blooming, it smelled like vanilla.

Once, right after I bought myself a little .410-gauge shotgun—it only cost twenty-seven dollars, it was my first earned money—I went hunting back in there. I was going to go sit for squirrels, hunting, yeah, but an easy hunt, mostly I was just going to be in that place, and the squirrels were an excuse.

After I'd been quiet for a few minutes, I heard something coming through the woods. I thought it might be a cow, but when I saw it, it was this man dressed in old-looking clothes with a big heavy leather satchel. He'd tote it a few steps and set it down and look behind him. Then he'd pick it up with the other hand and tote it a few more steps, set it down, turn around and look.

I sat still and he never saw me.

I don't know who he was or what he had in that satchel or anything about him, and there was no road back in there he was following. I don't know what he kept looking for behind him. I am sixty years old, I have never seen the same man again, and have wondered about him all these years. That man still drags that satchel through my dreams.

And I have always wondered what was in that old bag that was so very heavy.

Fire

Chota, Montana

A MAN: It was the Canyon Creek fire of '88, the fire had been burning in the Bob Marshall Wilderness and the forest service had the "let burn" policy, but the fire was big and there were ranchers that really didn't want to "let burn," because it was fixing to burn their property, and most local folks didn't think it was such a good idea either.

I'd ask once if they needed help and they'd said no.

They had a guy in there from Georgia who's biggest previous fire was four hundred acres, and this fire ate up 158 thousand acres in one night. They had a guy in there from New York who'd had a fire before with a thirty-mile-an-hour wind, but the wind that day had gusts to ninety. And they had a guy from Alaska who knew a lot about permafrost. And these guys were the fire bosses. A different one every day.

But that fire had blown up and they needed all the help they could get, so when I asked a second time, they said bring whatever I got and come up. I'd been working in Helena, I had a D-8 CAT on the back of my lowboy, I got there about five in the evening and we set up cutting another fire line. That is what you can do with a CAT.

The folks who were up there were people who had heavy equipment, people who owned property, farmers and ranchers who had had fire training, and anybody in three hundred miles who had a water truck. I know a Hotshot Crew chief, friend of mine, and she wouldn't take a crew in up here. They were using people with less than a week's training, a green crew, and she didn't want to be responsible for their lives. There were fires all over the west that summer, she didn't lack for work. This was the summer Yellowstone burned, too.

We had been working on the edge of hell, but by the third day we were in it. The Hotshot Crew chief had said, "If the fire rolls over you, safest place will be in the tractor. You'll get a little ambient heat but, it won't be too bad."

Well, my CAT was heating up because it had so much crap in the radiator, so I didn't dare stop it or it would have seized. My cousin walked over from another drainage, he'd followed my track up to where I was working.

"Fire's coming this way."

So I started trying to dig a hole to shelter the CAT—you sit six feet up, so I was thinking eight feet—but I hit solid rock in two feet. That's precious little shelter. So I started pushing all the brush around me away, so at least we'd be sitting in a clear space. We could feel it coming, a big fire is an ongoing explosion, you can feel it . . .

We got in the cab of the CAT and started pushing gloves or whatever into the holes so we could keep the fire out, but the wind blew them right back out. We had fire packs . . . Little coffin-sized space blankets. They have straps on all four corners and you're supposed to put your hands and feet in the four corners, lay flat on the ground and hold the thing over you, and hope it reflects enough heat that you live through it.

But I'm not there yet.

The thing that comes ahead of fire itself is embers, about the size of your fingers. They come in the fire storm. If a fire is big enough, it makes its own wind. Eighty, ninety miles an hour or more, and these embers ride the front of it. Embers were coming in the holes in the CAT's cabin, about to burn the pants off us, so we got those fire pack things and wrapped them around us . . .

And then the fire came . . .

A wall of flame broke over us. You'll take a little ambient heat . . . Man, ambient heat. We would have cooked without those little blankets.

I don't know how long it took, it was fast, we wouldn't have lived if it had been long, and fire uses oxygen, so along with the heat, there isn't much left to breathe . . .

And that's just the first wave. Everything that had been alive is now black and dead.

The second wave is not so bad—stuff is still burning, it is hot, but it is not blowing up like it does at first . . .

And then came the smoke . . .

It comes in colors: red, brown and white. Red is still reflecting the flame of the fire, brown was the real smoke, and white is when you could see sunlight through it again. We had to get out of the cab, the cab was a smokehouse itself by then.

We crawled to the ground I'd cleared trying to dig a hole for the CAT, it was rock, it was too hot, but we had to lay down on it to keep from breathing so much smoke. So we laid there, alive and roasting and counting our blessings.

When the smoke cleared a little, the Hotshot Crew chief came over and said, "Let's get out of here. We got some folks hurt."

It was the Hotshot Crew. They'd been on the ground with those space blankets and the fire had come through so fast they couldn't hold the blankets over them for the suction of the fire itself, and eight of them had their knees and elbows burnt pretty bad.

We beat that fire, but it took another two weeks and a half a million more acres, but that was the only time I was in it.

———

Thanks, Tom E.

———

Grabbler

East Tennessee

A MAN: My daddy was a grabbler. It is a way to catch fish. Grabbling is, in my opinion, the hard way to fish, except they caught a lot of fish that way. If they were catching fish to feed a bunch of people they went grabbling instead of fishing, my dad and a brother of his were good at it.

What you did was get wet.

You went in the water in a place you knew was likely to be good fishing, close to an overhanging rock, a hole you knew was there.

My daddy would sit in a little rowboat—he was looking for schools of fish—and he could be over the side of that boat so fast it was hard to believe, and he could stay down a long time. Daddy was a big man, lots of lung.

They wore their overalls when they were grabbling. It was what they did with the fish when they caught them, put them in the overalls.

I swear this is the truth: I've seen Daddy pop out of the water with a fish in each side pocket, a fish in each back pocket, a fish in the bib of his overalls, a fish in his mouth and one in each hand. Eight, if you're counting. And then, his brother with just as many. They could catch a mess of fish.

That was fishing schools.

They also grabbled for catfish—that was by over-hanging rocks or the places where they knew there were deeper holes in the water. I've seen my daddy run into a nest of snakes, and stand there and sling snakes out of the water and reach back into the same hole and come out with a fish.

My dad and his brother caught a ninety-pound catfish once, out of the Tennessee River. It took them both to get that fish. Ninety pounds is a lot of fish with no hook and line. It is a lot of fish with a hook and line. Daddy said it liked to have killed them both getting it out of the water. They tied it to the fender of the car to bring it home. Daddy didn't hunt. This would never have been a deer tied across his fender, but a really big catfish was a different story.

They hung that big catfish up down at the store, gutted it, skinned it, and gave everybody that wanted any some fish to take home. That's how Daddy did things. He never raised things just for us, never fished just for us, he fished for us and anybody else that wanted or needed it.

———

The grabbler is Dr. Jack Higgs's father. Jack tells the story of him.

Shot

Newport News, Virginia

A MAN: Ben Wilson got shot.

He had a little store out on pilings in the river, he'd load stuff onto his boat from our landing, take it out there, put it on shelves and sell it to the fishermen who stayed out all week. Nice little business.

And there was a mentally disturbed man out on the water. He fished sometimes, but sometimes he just sat in his boat and played russian roulette with this pistol he had. Sometimes he had bullets in it, but mostly not. He was scary. Ben was afraid of him. He'd lock up when that man came around because he didn't want him walking in the store on him with that gun.

Well, this day, Ben had scrubbed up the kitchen out there, had a bucket of wash water, and he went to the door, and he saw the man out there, but all he wanted to do was throw out the wash water, so he opened the door to do it. And bam. Right between the eyes with a .22. You couldn't have taken a pencil and located the spot any better than that guy hit.

Head wounds bleed bad and his blood just shot out.

Ben ran back inside and got a couple of towels, came back out and hollered at the man, "Throw that gun overboard!"

And the guy did it.

And Ben said, "Get that boat over here, you take me over to Powell's." And the guy did. Helped him right up to the house. Pop took him to the hospital. Later, Mother drove Mrs. Wilson to the hospital in the milk truck.

There were a couple of policemen who came, asked if I knew what happened, and I knew a little bit, and they asked if I had a boat to go out to the store. I had a rowboat. And they wanted to be rowed out there, and I did it. Fool thing to do, I mean that man was still out there—he'd gone back to the store after he got Ben to the house—and there I was with two policemen approaching in a rowboat. I didn't know whether he had another gun or not. He did sometimes. He was messing around in the store when we got there, eating crackers, and there were some other oystermen there, too, hanging around in their boats, watching. So I locked up the store and took Ben's boat back with me; me with this disturbed man and the two policemen.

Ben recovered completely with that bullet still in his head. First thing he did when he went back to the store— he had an old pair of oyster tongs—he went out and picked that gun right out of the water. He knew exactly where it was.

The disturbed man, well, Ben didn't charge him with anything, but they did lock him up. People had been afraid for a long time that he would do something to somebody and he had.

I don't know what became of him.

Ben had that bullet in his head for another thirty, almost forty years. Didn't bother him that anybody could see. They said it went in straight, between the left and right sides of the brain. A hair off either way would have killed him. Amazing grace.

Train Wreck

Etowah, Tennessee

A MAN: There are basically three ways to have a train wreck.

First: something is wrong with the tracks. A train can't run without tracks to run on; you lose the tracks, you're gonna wreck a train. Self-evident, and the most common problem.

That's why a section man's job is so important.

Ice can do it, ice can run a train off the tracks if it builds up right. Not real likely, but compacted ice can take a lot of weight, and all it has to do is get the first set of wheels aimed the wrong direction.

There was a wash, down close to Copperhill we knew to watch, track was almost always rough there, and we lost a train down there every once in a while.

Get out your section crews and your wreck crews. And you've got to have a crane to set the wreck on cars that are on the tracks once you get the tracks fixed. Hard, dangerous work, wrecks.

Second: if a train is going too fast around a curve, it can come off the tracks. This is momentum, and curves throw a whole different calculation into the momentum equation; it is the inclination of an object to go straight, not to curve.

We're in Isaac Newton's world here, not Einstein's universe. Train wheels are designed to hold the tracks, but it's part of the engineer's job to know how fast he can take a train around curves. If, for some reason the brakes have failed or are faulty—that used to be more of a problem than it is now—you can run into trouble the same way you can in a car going too fast on mountain roads.

Third: hit something. Mostly cars and cows. Neither of those things is going to really wreck a train. Trains are too big. Gonna be hard on the car or the cow. This is why trains have the right of way. Have to. Takes so long to stop. Too much you-know-what.

The way to have a really bad train wreck, and every trainman's nightmare is to meet another train coming at you on the same track. All that momentum is going to come to an abrupt halt the hard way. Two trains, rising up on impact like two strange dragons going at each other in waves of steam and fire.

It is not something human beings live to tell about. There was one of these on the L&N during WWI. Nobody lived through it, and nobody else likes to even think about it.

I had more of a taste than I wanted of a collision of trains. I was fireman, we were in the yard here at Etowah, and we were running a yard engine, we were on our way to pick up a load, and we were moving really slow. Yard speed. The brakeman hollered, and we saw another engine coming on a track that was going to cross ours, another yard engine, but he had a load behind him, he was moving at yard speed, too, so this wasn't fast at all, but we couldn't stop and he couldn't either.

And the steam and the fire, my God, it was the closest look at hell I've had yet. I jumped, there wasn't anything else to do. I got scratched up, this was a railroad yard and it was paved with cinders, but I was ok; brakeman jumped and broke ribs, and I kept looking for the engineer. He was a friend of mine. Now, this train we've hit hasn't stopped yet so every car that goes by keeps bumping us, so this whole mess is moving like it is alive.

I saw a bull once that had gone rabid, it was unusual, but it happened every once in a while, and this animal wasn't noted for his good temper to begin with, and my father had to shoot him. He had taken two shots to his head, but he was not down yet, and he was still trying to take something—anything—to the next life with him. I had never seen anything so dangerous.

Our little yard engine was like that bull, it was destroyed, but it wasn't down yet, fire and steam still shooting out of it. I went back into it to get my friend, he was burned bad with steam, his skin was ready to split, but I got him out.

So you've been waiting for your train wreck story, there it is. Not a big train wreck. But people don't live through big ones—nobody left to tell about them.

Wasted Youth

Southeast Georgia

Part One

AN OLDER MAN: I wasted my youth on Crooked River, that's what I tell people. I say it because it is funny, but the truth is, my youth wasn't wasted. From the time it got warm enough in the spring till it got cold in the fall, my cousin and I would set up a camp back on my father's land and live in it, and hunt or fish. This was weekends till the end of the school year and all summer, and then weekends again in the fall. We did this from the time we were eleven, twelve, through high school, and for years after whenever we could.

For a while, we were as close to being feral as you can be and still get by in what passed for civilized society out on Crooked River. We could sit down at my mother's dinner table and eat with a fork and knife, but we sure weren't much for polite conversation.

We hunted. We took alligators, sold the skin, got about fifteen cents a foot, that's the belly skin, nobody wanted the rest of it. Too tough to work. We caught the little ones alive and sold them. It was probably some of the baby alligators

I caught that ended up in the sewers of New York City. And snakes. There was a fellow who bought live snakes, had roadside attraction out on the old highway, and he'd buy what we caught. Poisonous snakes brought the most, so we looked for rattlers and cottonmouths. Caught them by the hundreds. We hunted the gators and snakes for money. We fished and hunted everything else for food for the family table and our own food in camp. It was a wonderful life. Couldn't have happened anywhere but here. It is a special place where fresh water runs into salt water.

PART TWO

AN OLDER MAN: There are a lot of things to say about hunting. The first to talk about and get it over with is the act of killing something that is alive. I don't feel the same way about it that I used to. When I was young and immortal, I could do it without thinking much about it. I was raised on a farm. Animals were fattened and slaughtered, and my family and I ate them. It was food. Killing something in the woods was easier, I had no relationship with those animals, and killing a big alligator was like doing everything else a favor.

But now I am older and not so immortal. And I want to say that everything, everything struggles towards life. Nothing gives up life easy. That includes old men. And hunting is first and foremost about taking life.

Used to be a passage towards manhood for a boy was his daddy taking him out hunting, and he killed a boar or a deer. "Killed his first buck at ten." My daddy said that of me and I spent a lot of years proud of it.

The thing to say on our behalf: we weren't wasteful, we ate what we killed.

I've seen men go into the woods and shoot and not even bother to bring home what died. Or killing something that's been in a cage, and just been let out to get shot. They were there for the pleasure of taking life. Lord help us, when did that get to be a man's pleasure?

Know this: life doesn't quit easy. There are more or less efficient ways to kill things, but life does not ever quit without a fight. And to kill anything, you have to make yourself immune to something else's fight. We live the bloodiest paradox I ever run onto: to stay alive in this world, we have to eat things which have been alive and we have to take the life of them to eat them. The difference between us and the gators, is that we do the animals we eat the courtesy of killing them before we eat them, which seems to me like a real courtesy if you've ever seen a gator take something. But I am less and less immune to that struggle towards life, I value any life at all more, the closer I come to being at the end of my own. I know the way of this world is the death of the body, but I'm having a harder time than I ever imagined justifying even so small a killing as a mousetrap in my pantry. If an owl gets Miss Mousey, that is her bad luck, but she is food, she contributes to life ongoing. If she dies in my trap, she is trash. Even a mouse should not be trash.

Part Three

AN OLDER MAN: I'm probably from the last generation in this country that is ever going to get to be really at home in these or any woods. My grandchildren can visit woods, but they cannot live in them, not like I did. I know what I did in my father's woods is part of why the alligators needed protecting, but alligators have made quite a recovery and I don't regret the snakes, never has been any shortage of them. But the mullet you don't see jumping anymore and the shrimp and crabs that just aren't here anymore, and then the wild turkey and the bear and the boar . . . nobody understood. Things were just available for the taking. Dominion. If you go back and translate that passage in the Bible from the original Aramaic or Hebrew or whatever it was, "dominion" is just one meaning of the word, it can also mean man was given charge of protecting animals. I didn't do much protecting.

But here's the other side. Real hunting teaches things. One is how to live with your own mind in silence, another is patience, a third is how to see what is there instead of what you think ought to be there. Best way to go hungry in the woods is to look for what you think you ought to find. Another thing it teaches: how to choose your moment and act on it, and not quit just because something gets hard to do. That's not all, that's just what I think offhand . . . So tell me where my grandchildren and their children can learn these things. That's what we got to figure out, how we can teach this kind of learning along with all the book learning. I like book learning, I read a lot, but the real education of this world isn't in books.

Hermaphrodite

Chicago, Illinois

One story told by a Man and a Woman.

BOTH: I was born July 7, 1947,

WOMAN: a girl child with all her fingers and toes. My aunts were told I was quite perfect, and I was hauled off to the nursery like happens to babies in hospitals, and in passing the first stool, the baby's first stool, the meconium—it even has a name because it is sometimes hard for the newborn child to pass—in passing the first stool,

MAN: a penis popped out.

WOMAN: The doctors said,

BOTH: "Your child is both a boy and a girl, you have a choice."

WOMAN: Some choice, in a culture that values boy children more than girls.

MAN: "A boy," my mother said, "William Lloyd." And so they sewed up the vaginal opening and left the penis, and sent me home to grow up male with no more thought of it.

WOMAN: But I was not a male.

MAN: We had a big, brown, leather-covered footstool, and I would sit on it in front of a bay window where I could see

my reflection and comb my hair, and when my parents
asked what I was doing, I said,

WOMAN: "I'm going to grow up and be a beautiful woman."

MAN: "No, Son—"

WOMAN: they were horrified—

MAN: "You are a boy, you will be a man." Well, I had the right
plumbing,

WOMAN: but not the right heart.

MAN: Once, I was playing—we had a big dining-room table,

WOMAN: I made my playhouse under it, and stuffed my pants
with newspaper like I was pregnant—my mother was pregnant again at the time, and I played like I was cooking supper for my husband who was coming home to eat it.

MAN: I was not allowed this game.

WOMAN: My mother yanked the stuffing from my belly.

MAN: "You are the man, you go to work and come home to your
wife who cooks you supper. Play that!"

WOMAN: But I did not like that.

MAN: My father decided to teach me to box,

WOMAN: and slapped me hard when I did not want to do it.

MAN: Life with my parents was like that. Plenty of slaps and
punches.

WOMAN: At ten, eleven, I began developing breasts. I will
not describe those years, I don't even like to think about
them.

MAN: Think of going to boy's gym class with a penis and developing breasts if you want to know what they were like.
Think of laying in bed at night with pubescent wet dreams

WOMAN: and budding breasts. Just think of it.

MAN: If you can.

WOMAN: I wondered if I was human.

MAN: But how could I be more human, how much more human
could a body get than to be both male

WOMAN: and female?

MAN: I think there are a variety of hells on this earth

BOTH: and I lived through one of them.

WOMAN: I ran away from home at sixteen, and at nineteen I went to California, and I got involved with a gender-identification group, and I had the vagina opened again,

MAN: but I chose to keep what God had given me, so I did not have the penis taken off.

WOMAN: And I fell in love and married. I hadn't thought that it would be possible for me.

MAN: He told his mother we could hunt and fish

WOMAN: and turn around and make love.

MAN: I was truly happy.

WOMAN: But my husband was a drug dealer, and he was shot in the eye, but he didn't die immediately. He lost everything but his life until he finally lost his life, too. His mother told me to take the money we had and go somewhere else.

MAN: I went back to Iowa,

WOMAN: and I entered nursing school, and spent the money towards an RN degree,

MAN: and ran out of money before I had the degree,

WOMAN: and, with the help of a "cousin,"

MAN: I was turning tricks.

WOMAN: I had certain exotic

MAN: and erotic attributes

WOMAN: nobody else on the street could match.

MAN: I got an RN degree.

WOMAN: I went to Des Moines to take the state boards for certification. I turned tricks for money for the motel and food, studied between them, and got up the next morning and took more of the tests.

MAN: I did quite well on the tests.

WOMAN: I came to Chicago and got a job.

MAN: A registered nurse. But people were . . .

WOMAN: There was a Christmas party and, yes, I drank too much.

MAN: I needed people to know who I was, so I named myself what I am.

BOTH: Hermaphrodite.

WOMAN: People are not always kind when they find out you're different.

MAN: These were all medical people

WOMAN: and they said . . .

MAN: they said, "We see you in a different light now."

WOMAN: That is not what they said.

MAN: But nursing work got hard to come by.

WOMAN: So I started hustling again.

BOTH: My attributes,

WOMAN: those very things that were so troubling to my co-workers,

MAN: were very helpful on the street.

WOMAN: There are people who prefer

MAN: such originals as I am.

WOMAN: I lived with a series of men who took me in. Pimps, some of them.

MAN: I got addicted to cocaine.

WOMAN: The drug made it easier to do what had to be done. My cousin, my pimp—he started demanding more money, as a pimp often does, and I'd stay out for the extra fifty dollars . . .

MAN: so I could go back in and take my shower and sleep in peace.

WOMAN: I married again to get away from that pimp. My second husband died violently, too.

MAN: I had an uncle in my family,

WOMAN: the only one of any of them who was good to me. He watched out for me when he could. Sometimes I stayed with him. One night he was playing pool with a man named Joe. He'd lost his money, so he laid the keys to his apartment down on the pool table and played for those, and lost them, too, and I met my third husband when Joe came through the door that night. We lived together twenty-one years. He died last spring of AIDS.

BOTH: And I have it.

MAN: It will be AIDS that kills me

WOMAN: and not a customer.

MAN: I always thought it would be a customer.

WOMAN: You live through stuff or with stuff. Mostly, I've lived
with this body. Now, I have AIDS and I won't live through
that. I have sold myself for money and I have been loved
and I know the difference. I feel more female now

MAN: than male,

WOMAN: so I've named myself Willa Lorene

MAN: instead of William Lloyd,

BOTH: but I have lived on both sides of sex in one life.

Bad Days and
Hard Comedy

Tour of a Minor Traffic
Altercation

Port Gibson, Mississippi

Narrator, Vodka Man (middle-aged), Vodka Man's Mother, Driver and Passenger of the second car, Sober Witness, Porchman and a Truck Driver. The Narrator should have something lawyerly about him; it was a lawyer who told the original story.

All these people are on stage in different places. The Narrator tours the stage to get to those people who have a part in each section. So this piece is not actually a tour of a traffic altercation, it is the tour of a telling about a traffic altercation. It should take the whole stage by various moments, and as much as can be made of the tour should be.

PART ONE

NARRATOR (*Like he/she was making opening remarks in front of a jury; to us*): This is the step-by-step re-creation of a minor traffic altercation reenacted to clarify the events for those of us who seek information, clarification and edification on the subject.

VODKA MAN: Mother! MOTHER! The garage just called and it is time to check the oil in the automobile. I'll be back when I'm done.

MOTHER *(From off)*: I thought you just got the oil checked last Monday.

VODKA MAN: That was the steering fluid last Monday.

MOTHER: Be careful, it's hot out already, and you're sensitive . . .

VODKA MAN: Mother, I'm not that sensitive . . .

MOTHER: Just wear your hat, so when you come back in you don't have to lie down and you can keep me company while Lilly fixes dinner . . .

NARRATOR: Now, the garage has called this man and told him that the case of vodka he ordered from the bootlegger has arrived and they'd be grateful if he'd come and pick it up now. The garage didn't want to have to hold it, the town of Port Gibson was *dry*, and a particular sheriff's deputy had been less than satisfied with some mechanical work the garage had done on his personal car, and he had been making an uncomfortable noise about the fellow he thought might be a bootlegger—he knew the bootlegger as well as anybody else—stopping at that particular garage on a mighty regular basis. Monday morning, to be specific. So the garage had promised to redo the mechanical work for free with a new part instead of a rebuilt one, but, in the meantime, the new part is on back order, the deputy was impatient, and garage people did not want a Monday morning case of vodka just sitting around. It is a perfectly good way to go to jail in a dry town, to get caught trafficking in bootleg liquor. So they'd called the man who wanted it, to come and get it. He'd been expecting the call. Gets one every Monday morning. "The lubrication you ordered is here." Just in case anybody was listening in on the telephone, it was phrased in automotive terms. He used to wait to get it till his mother took her afternoon nap. That was easier, no explanation going out the door, but now they want him to come and get the lubrication immediately. So he goes. He drives the biggest blackest Lincoln they make during the whole sixties, and that car has the biggest engine Ford ever put in an automobile under its hood. Drives it down to the garage. Backs in. Opens the hood and the trunk. Somebody looks under the hood while somebody else puts the lubrication in the trunk. All but one bottle. That is the lubrication that goes into the driver. Before he gets home. Makes him so sensitive to the sun that he has to lie down when he gets home. Every time. Hat or no hat. Now, he takes that big Lincoln and he drives out into the country to test the lubrication, because he knows he cannot do it at home with Mother awake, and he has no intention of waiting till after dinner. When he comes back into town, it is not quite dinnertime, he is very well lubricated himself, and he is driving north on College Street. Driving south on College Street are two other gentlemen who accepted delivery from the bootlegger that morning, and also tested the lubrication, and they are coming at one another as drunks do: they are moving slowly, but every time they look at one another they end up pointed at one another, so they both look away and hop the curb. And then they got to get back in the street again, so they end up looking at one another, and it turns out that when driver A, in the Lincoln, passes driver B with passenger C, in a Chevrolet, he scrunches a fender.

PART TWO

NARRATOR *(To us)*: You remember the scrunch and how we got there? It was a fender-bender, and not much of that, 'cause everybody was going so slow. It was on College Street at the annex of the Presbyterian church. But it so panicked the driver of the Lincoln that he floored the gas on that 350-horsepower engine, and that car tried its best to go into orbit. It climbed an embankment, swerved just before it hit the Presbyterian annex, turned and came down the sidewalk, down the concrete steps of the annex sidewalk, jumped that curb, crossed the street, missing the other car, climbed the embankment on the other side. We know all this because there was a sober witness, she was sitting on her front porch when the accident happened, but she ceases to be unbiased at this point . . .

SOBER WITNESS: I was sure I was dead, that big old black car headed right at me . . . *(Covers her head with an apron)*

NARRATOR: It missed the porch by inches, went back down the embankment, hopped the curb, crossed the street again, missing the second car again, all this at top speed, mind you, hopped the curb on the other side, took out a small tree, and ran dead center into the side of the Presbyterian church.

(To the Sober Witness) You can look.

(She does.)

Would you please describe what you saw next.

SOBER WITNESS: That big old car trying to go in the church through a hole in the wall.

NARRATOR: And . . .

SOBER WITNESS: Well, it finally quit trying to get all the way in the church.

NARRATOR: Yes.

SOBER WITNESS: And the driver opened his door—see the front part of the car was on the inside of the church, so when he got out—

NARRATOR: You can see all this from your front porch?

SOBER WITNESS: I certainly could. It was a big hole.

NARRATOR: And what did he do?

SOBER WITNESS: He threw something back outside in the bushes.

NARRATOR: And then what did he do?

SOBER WITNESS: He laid down in the Presbyterian church and went to sleep.

NARRATOR: There are those who say he passed out, spread-eagled, on the floor in front of the altar.

SOBER WITNESS: I was very surprised, I didn't even know he was a Presbyterian.

PART THREE

PORCHMAN: You again? You are taking up an awful lot of time with a single incident of bad driving.

NARRATOR: But this is the South . . .

PORCHMAN: What's that got to do with it? You going on and on about a fool drunk and a minor car wreck.

NARRATOR: Wait a minute. This is how stories are told and retold. It is an art to turn a story like this to true comedy. People have had to excuse themselves from the dinner table they were laughing so hard when I've told this story.

PORCHMAN: Didn't realize I was interrupting Picasso.

NARRATOR: Will Rogers. That's the tradition.

PORCHMAN: I got no problem with art, friend, I just got trouble spending art on a sorry drunk and a car wreck.

NARRATOR: I didn't know it was just a drunk and a car wreck. I thought it was the web of life in a small place, character weaknesses, the vagaries of law and order, the knowing that comes with genuine experience of human fallibility, and the problem with Presbyterians.

PORCHMAN: Could a fooled me.

NARRATOR *(To us)*: The hole in the side of the Presbyterian church began to attract a crowd. The driver of the Lincoln was unstirred. He lay on the floor like he belonged there. The sober witness . . .

SOBER WITNESS: I told the sheriff what I had seen flying off into the bushes.

NARRATOR: . . . and the sheriff found the vodka bottle and suspected the incident might be "alcohol related." He wrote that on his report. The sheriff roused the Lincoln driver . . .

VODKA MAN: What? What? Where am I?

SOBER WITNESS: I don't think you want to know. I especially don't think you want your mother to know.

NARRATOR: There was a truck driver who had been passing and had seen the Lincoln trying to launch itself . . .

TRUCK DRIVER: I want to know who was driving that car.

VODKA MAN: No one. No one at all. It was wheeling itself.

NARRATOR: Now, about this time, the gentleman and his passenger, who had been in the car the Lincoln hit, showed up . . .

VODKA MAN: Oh, you! I am sorry, I am so very sorry, so very, very sorry . . .

SECOND CAR DRIVER: Aw, hush, we seen it was you, we knew it was Monday morning, we had plenty of chance to turn off, and we didn't do it.

NARRATOR: On the strength of that statement, these two fellows (and not the one with the nose of his Lincoln in the side of the church) were given the ticket for careless driving. Nobody looked in the trunk of the Lincoln either, so this man had himself an extended episode of acute sensitivity and spent most of the next week unable to get out of bed. But he was up and driving again the next Monday morning. The Lincoln was somewhat the worse for wear but damage was cosmetic not mechanical, and those 350 horses, every single one of them, was as willing as ever to get that lubrication.

———

You'll find Porchman's story elsewhere in this book, Porchman/ Parchman.

Snake-Bit Dog

Belle Glade, Florida

Three teenage boys.

1: There were three of us:
2: we were thirteen, fourteen and fifteen years old.
1: And we were bored,
3: really bored.
1: We'd done chores.
3: Boring.
1: We'd tormented my sisters.
2: Really boring.
1: We'd ridden the cows.
3: Boring.
2: Goring if you're not careful
1: and a real problem if Daddy caught you doing it.
2: So we decided to go hunting.
3: We decided to go kill something.
1: Let's go kill something.
2: Between us, we had a .22 single-shot rifle.
1: Legitimately owned, last year's Christmas present,
3: and a .32 pistol.
1: Borrowed.

2: Stolen.

3: I took it back.

2: Your daddy found it first.

1: We took my dog,

2: can't go hunting without a dog,

3: except that dog couldn't tree a squirrel.

2: Still can't go hunting without a dog.

1: We took a half gallon of water for three of us,

2: turns out, that's not much,

3: not near enough,

1: and pulled some onions out of the vegetable garden as we left the farm.

3: Why'd we take those onions?

1: I don't know.

2: We could have made ham sandwiches.

1: But we didn't.

3: Bunch of onions.

1: No pot to cook in.

2: Nobody's going to *cook* anything.

1: We were headed for the piney woods, a few miles out.

2: The minute we got off the land cleared for the farm it was custard apple,

3: then about a half a mile of wallows,

2: then about a quarter of a mile of elderberry,

3: then we were into saw grass.

1: Now, none of this is easy going.

2: Custard apple you have to go under, the wallows you have to go over,

3: elderberry, well, they're thick and you sort of go through,

2: and then saw grass can cut boot leather if it gets it at the right angle.

1: Now, along about the elderberry, the dog got bit by a water moccasin.

2: You don't know that.

1: He got bit by something, he had two little holes in his paw. That's snake bite if ever I knew it.

2: It could have been a rattlesnake.

1: He would have known a rattlesnake and left it alone.

2: Not if he stepped on it first.

1: Ok. He got bit by a snake, probably a water moccasin.

3: Dog's gonna die.

1: Shut up.

2: We wrapped the dog's paw up in a handkerchief so he could stand to put it on the ground,

1: and kept going, the dog still with us.

2: Got out to the elders, and there was a hole, and a big old gator in it.

3: You ought to feed that dog to him, dog's gonna die, you could put him out of his misery right now.

2: Instead, we shot the gator.

1: We didn't just shoot him,

3: we pulled a ten-foot alligator out of his hole,

2: tail first, which is not the smart way to do it,

1: not that there is a real smart way to do it,

2: so we could shoot him.

1: Something to kill, and my dog was snake bit.

2: It would be illegal now, but it wasn't then,

3: it was something to do.

1: And of course, one .22 bullet didn't kill it.

3: That thing was . . .

2: That may be the most dangerous thing any of us ever did, putting the first bullet in that alligator.

1: By the time it was dead, we didn't even take the hide.

3: We left him laying.

2: We might not ought to have done that.

3: It might have killed us if we hadn't.

1: It was dead.

3: We had to kill it, it could have come out of that hole and chased us.

1: Right.

2: So next, we came to a cypress head,

3: and even the snake-bit dog smelled something,

1: and when we looked up in the tree, we couldn't tell what it was,

2: so we shot it anyway,

3: and down fell a big raccoon.

1: We did keep that hide.

2: Now, we've been out for a while,

1: we've eaten the onions,

3: the half gallon of water is gone,

1: my dog is snake bit,

3: but we'd shoot the raccoon.

2: We can cook it.

1: So we built a fire and tried to cook that raccoon.

2: Now, most the time when you are cooking a raccoon, you boil it,

1: throw that first water away,

2: way away,

1: as far away as you can get it,

2: boil it again

1: and throw that water away, too,

2: and use the meat in a stew with lots of other stuff.

3: Raccoon is strong flavor.

1: Gamey.

2: Real gamey.

3: Extra real, genuine, blue-ribbon, foul-tasting, gut-turning, carrion-smelling gamey.

2: And tough.

3: Chewy like shoe leather might be chewy. Except I never ate any shoe leather.

1: And we were out of water.

2: We were on dry land by then,

3: but water is never far below ground here.

1: So we dug a hole

2: and put the handkerchief from the dog's paw,

3: snake-bit dog,

1: sick dog.

2: Put the handkerchief over the end of the jug to strain the water.

1: Then put the handkerchief back on the dog's paw.

2: Drank every bit of the water.

3: And ate that raccoon.

1: And so nourished and refreshed,

2: we headed on towards the lake.

1: But there had been a fire,

3: that's how people clear land here,

1: and the ground was still hot

2: and smoking,

1: and we had to get across this mess on logs that were down,

2: and hot

3: and smoking,

1: and when we got to the lake, we just waded in

3: and stood there for a while.

2: Long time.

1: My feet are still hot.

2: So now, we're wet, too.

3: Where are we?

2: I don't know.

1: That's the lake.

2: *Tom Fool genius.*

3: So we sat around for a while,

2: heard a train, and found the railroad track,

3: then found a crossing we knew about six miles from home.

1: I don't feel very good.

3: Yeah, and your dog's snake bit.

1: I really don't feel very good. I think I'm gonna—

3: GO IN THE BUSHES AND DO IT!

2: This dog's not going too good either.

3: Really sick dog.

2: And there is six miles to get home.

1: I think I'm gonna die.

2: You can't.

1: I can if I want to.

3: Can you walk?

1: No.

3: Can you crawl?

1: No.

2: You mean we got to carry you?

1: No. Just leave me alone. I can die by myself.
2: We can't do that.
3: Let's vote.

> *(The voter, 3, gets a truly dirty look. 1 is hoisted onto the back of 2 and they start out, but the dog can't do it.)*

1: Somebody has to carry the dog.

> *(So 3 picks up the dog.)*

2: Six miles.
3: Snake-bit dog.
2: Five miles.
1: I gotta go to the bushes again.
3: I think I gotta go to the bushes, too.
2: Lucky break: a ride for two miles.
1: He could have taken us on home.
2: He didn't have the gas.
1: Three miles to go.
3: Snake-bit dog.

> *(1 is making noises again.)*

2: You got to go to the bushes again?
3: Two miles to go.
2: I'm glad you're losing weight instead of putting it on.
3: Another ride for one mile.
2: One mile to go.
3: Snake-bit dog.
2: We got home.

> *(The sick boy, 1, and his snake-bit dog are dumped unceremoniously. 2 and 3 exit.)*

1: The dog and I both lived, but that's how I lost my taste for snake venom ground water, raccoon meat, and alligator killing all in the same day.

———

I've written plays for several places where snakes and alligators mean more than they do where I live. You can find rattlesnakes and copperheads in the mountains around where I live, but not very likely in my backyard. And alligators aren't here at all. I'm grateful. A friend in St. Mary's, Georgia, can't let her cats outside her house because of the alligators that live in the lovely little lake in her gated subdivision. Belle Glade, Florida; Colquitt, Georgia; and Walton County, Florida—other places I have worked—are the same story. Most people don't fish golf balls out of water traps on golf courses in any of those places, because you likely put yourself in close proximity to creatures who consider you (or your arm or leg) the perfect lunch.

Both snakes and alligators are primal creatures in human imagination, so when you go collecting stories, i.e., people's memories, in places where those creatures share the territory, you get stories about them.

I use some of them because they are so primal. You'll find more than one "snake and alligator" reference in this book. Mostly, I add levity so that the s&a business has some comedy added to its danger. I've even written an alligator chorus (for St. Mary's, Georgia) that sings praises for things it loves . . .

Thanks for the poodles,
thanks for the rats,
thanks for the cats,
thanks for the mud . . .

CRUNCH!

Thanks for the fish,
thanks for the snakes,
thanks for the poodles,
thanks for the chickens . . .

CRUNCH!

Thanks for the arms,
thanks for the legs,
thanks for the people,
and their dumb little pets . . .

———

Alligator: When we can find them.

CRUNCH!

Etcetera. I do that, because just evoking fear of the s&a contingent doesn't serve much.

    And then, I love the comedy, so I go for it.

Work

Cooking Liquor

Harlan, Kentucky

A YOUNG WOMAN: My daddy cooked liquor and sold it whole-
sale, left it to somebody else to distribute. Went armed
every day of his life. He was actually more dangerous as he
got older, even after he quit cooking he felt venerable. A
couple of folks up our holler got killed 'cause somebody
tried to rob them, probably for money for drugs, that's a
big problem here now, and that wasn't gonna happen to
Daddy. So he went armed.

He always used mules to pack his supplies back in to his
still and then to deliver his "product" to his wholesalers.
He never was his own distributor. "That's how to get
caught." If you were fool enough to come to our house
looking for liquor, he might give you a drink or two from
his fence-post stash if you were a friend, keep you feeling
good, but he never sold it from home. Never.

And he never delivered to anybody but his "distributor"
out in the middle of the woods somewhere, in the middle
of the night. He was smart about it.

Still got caught. Went to trial three times, but no jury
would convict him. He was too good a citizen, too honest
and generous a man, and nobody except the feds—federal

agents: Alcohol, Tobacco and Firearms, ATF—nobody but them saw cooking homemade liquor as such a crime. The IRS that might get you, too, if they knew you were selling it. Untaxed income. That's what put Al Capone in prison.

Got us a story around here lately about somebody the feds tried to get on untaxed income, a bootlegger, not a cooker, and turns out she'd been overpaying her taxes for years. I laughed on that till I choked . . .

Some folks back then, probably now too, saw the whole enterprise as a sin, but a sin was between you and God, not you and the government.

I'm of kindly mixed vision on the federal stuff. It was federal intervention that finally let the unions organize, and the government's war on poverty here in the sixties did some real good. Wasn't ever steak and potatoes, but food's food when you're hungry. Lots of folks back in Daddy's day didn't like government at all, and didn't see much difference between one set of feds and another.

Saw them as butting in much too much where they had no business.

There is history here, the National Guard coming in to bust strikes that shouldn't have been busted. I'm not saying the troubles were ever a good idea, but . . . Well, it was hard for a man to feel good about a situation in which a mule was more valuable than he was. You used to hear that. If a mule got killed in a mine, they had to buy another one; if a man got killed, all they had to do was hire another, so the mule was more valuable. There were some long years of that kind of thinking, that kind of hard living here. And you live with that long enough, well . . . just say some folks saw bucking the feds as a kind of dangerous sport. That was true of my daddy. Mama, too, I think.

He cooked good stuff. He was clean about it. First problem of cooking liquor was good water. The feds hunted along the creeks, so you didn't want to set up your still on a creek, it was gonna get busted if you did that, and you were likely to get caught.

Daddy looked for crawdad holes, said that wherever you found crawdad holes, there is water not far below the ground, so he'd look for crawdad holes and dig, set himself up a little pond, with a pipe run downhill of it.

Now this is a lot of work.

Then you had to have fuel for your fire. You wanted wood that had been down and dead for a while; green wood smokes, so you wanted dry wood. You made your pond and then you start walking the territory around for down wood.

This was another way they could find you—if they come onto a place in the woods that's cleaned of down wood, somebody had been cleaning it. You couldn't ever cut a bunch of trees and stack them to dry, because somebody would notice that.

So, after you've cleaned a space out of dead wood, you've got to go hunting for another place to find good water and set up all over again.

A lot of work.

Now, cooking in the day, if you didn't have dry wood, was a problem 'cause of the smoke. And cooking at night, somebody could see the light from the fire if you weren't real careful about it. Sometimes when he was using smoky wood, Mama would set up her washpot fire down in the yard with the greenest stuff she could burn and make a lot of smoke coming from the yard. And somebody would almost always come sneaking around to look at who might be cooking what, and find that washpot fire, and go back home.

If that didn't work . . . we'd had a dog got killed, Rattler, and Mama would send us younguns out hollering for Rattler. "He's a big mean dog, let me get him up before he hurts you . . ." And there'd be a bunch of us children out yelling like crazy for Rattler, and sound carries in these hollers. That was Daddy's signal to pack up and go somewhere else . . .

I never saw my father drunk. I'm sure he got that way sometimes, I heard some stories. I never saw him mean to us or to Mama or to his animals. I've seen him stand up for himself, hold that gun on somebody he didn't want going on up the mountain. More than once, I've seen that.

He put us younguns through school cooking liquor. Quit the business when we were on our own. My brothers went to trade schools, some of my sisters and I made teachers.

It was Mama's idea we had to go on to school, and the liquor was how to do it. She didn't want Daddy or her sons in the mines, men died underground, and whatever it took to stay aboveground—even at the risk of some months in jail—was a risk she could live with.

———

Cooking liquor, in some fashion or another, is an occupation that shows up with astonishing consistency in the sets of community stories that cross my desk, and, yes, a few people do still do it. Do you know what I'm talking about when I mention a ring of pearls? I've even seen one story (all the players have already gone to their reward) in which the moonshiners and the feds were members of the same family, a couple were moonshiners and ATF agents, and when the government started pressuring their employees to catch somebody, the family determined who had the oldest still that could be busted up with no real loss, and then drew straws to see who was going to get caught at that still, with the provision that everyone else would take care of the short straw's family while he was in jail.

We have an ongoing romance with this sort of outlaw business, so I've included this story because it reflects some of this romance, but this one speaks a little more of the realities than most do.

People who buy moonshine now are buying that romance, and likely paying for rather rough liquor (rarely aged, the cooker doesn't want it in his possession any longer than it has to be there) cooked in somebody's basement over gas rings from tap water, refined sugar and commodity corn, and they are looking for that illusive ring of bubble pearls they've heard about that is supposed to form when you shake a mason jar of good corn liquor. There is a market because it is outside the law. You can buy the same stuff at the liquor store, guaranteed aged less than thirty days, and it won't give you the jake leg. We do nurture our little illegalities. We seem to like them a lot. Maybe we need them. We certainly hold on to them. And where there is a market, there is guaranteed to be a product.

Route

Lancaster, Pennsylvania

A YOUNG MAN: A snow story, a blizzard, it is a story that changed my life, and made me the explosive acquaintance of one Delbert Howes.

My father had a contract to deliver mail and newspapers—he drove a truck, his route was twenty-three little towns around here, and he'd get the mail from the post office and the papers to a drop-off point and head on to the next. Once a day, Sunday included for the newspapers. The job started in the middle of the night, he'd pick up papers as they came off the press and—if I remember—he'd go by the post office when he got back from his newspaper round and pick up the mail to deliver the next day. He owned his own truck, did most of the work on it himself, so he was an independent, self-sufficient sort of man. And we have some snow here, so he was pretty well equipped for snow. His truck sat high off the ground, had tires for snow, or maybe it was chains, I don't remember, but he was used to doing it. A little snow didn't bother him.

Now, this is the man who'd told me my first year of high school that it was time I started pulling some of my own weight and to get a job. I had jobs all through high school, nothing I particularly liked, except working at a green-house (I liked messing with the flowers), but that was the job that paid the worst of anything I did. Of course. So I had had jobs, and I had another job of my own the morning he woke me up and said it had snowed, and he thought he might need a little help to do the route.

Could I come along?

Snowed. It was a terrible blizzard and it was still coming down.

What you have to know is that my father got paid for the day if he tried it, he could get stuck and not make it all the way, but he got paid if he tried, and he didn't get paid if he sat at home for weather or sickness or anything else. So he was determined to try. We drove the trolley tracks out of town because they'd been cleared. We got out to the highway, and there were these little black nubs sticking up by the side of the road and that was fence posts. And snow was still coming. It wasn't long before we were shoveling and pushing and whatever else we could do to make a mile. Then, a few yards. It was awful. And cold, it was ferociously cold and windy.

We got to the first stop, got stuck a hundred times doing it, he was driving, but most of the time I was out front with a shovel, and there were times we were both out front with a shovel making tracks for the truck to roll in.

My father said when we get to Delbert Howes's house, Delbert was an acquaintance of his, that we'll rouse him up and see if we can't go in and get warm. It was about six in the morning by then, and we were really cold. We finally get to Delbert Howes's, and banged on his door. Delbert was up already but barely. He had on this long heavy woolly nightshirt and he was surprised to see us at his front door. But he let us in, and, yeah, he could get us warm. He'd not got his stove going good yet though—he'd just gotten out of bed. He threw a couple of sticks of kindling in it, but that didn't do anything to speak of, so he went over to a corner and pumped about a quarter of a dipper of kerosene from a little pump, and came back and threw that onto the hot coals.

My father and I headed for the door when we first realized he was going to dump the kerosene in the stove. When it hit the hot coals, we were blown through the door. Delbert was scorched, all the woolly nap was burnt right off his fancy nightshirt and his beard caught fire. He was still putting it out when we came back in.

We helped close up the stove again. It was heating pretty fast by then, made sure Delbert was ok, and he was, and headed back into the cold. Lord only knew what Delbert might try next, and we didn't want to be there to witness. Outside, it was more of the same. To make the long story short, it took us more than sixteen hours to go less than fourteen miles, that's seven miles out, seven miles back.

When I got home, I went down in the basement of that house to where the furnace was, it was warm and dark, and I took off all my clothes and sat on a bench. I was there a long time. I was telling myself, I want to make my living some other way. I want to work where it is warm, and where I won't die if my back gives out.

I hadn't really thought about going to college until then, there naked on the bench in the dark and the warm. I'd always just assumed I'd eventually find a job I could live with, and live with it. That's what everybody else seemed to do.

It was exactly what my father had done, but until that day, I had no idea how hard my father's life could be. That day was awful and dangerous. We had to dig out of twenty-foot drifts. So my father could get paid for trying.

I decided to see if there was a school that would take me, where I could work for my tuition, and get a college education. I got dressed and went upstairs to my room, and that night I wrote the first letters of inquiry. I looked out my window at the snow and wrote the best letters I could think of.

It was a blizzard that made a teacher of me. I like indoor work in the winter.

Hard Way to Hunt

Colquitt, Georgia

A MAN: It was back during the Depression, and money, well, you didn't see any money at all, and my daddy was farming on shares, and the fellow he was farming for didn't want us keeping animals. Keeping animals was a way to get a little ahead, and this fellow didn't want us ahead, he wanted us right where we were.

So we hunted to make up meat to eat. We were poor enough then we didn't have a gun or the money to buy one, but we had a dog, a good dog, and you could hunt some things with a good dog.

You turned the dog loose hungry, and you followed him.

If the dog treed something, you'd cut the tree down, and hold the dog to keep him out of the way of the falling tree and then let him go in time to catch whatever the critter was, and then you had to get the dog and the critter and separate them and kill whatever the critter was.

It was the hard way to hunt, but you do a lot of stuff the hard way if you're hungry.

I was nine or ten, somewhere in there, and my daddy and granddaddy decided it was time I went with them, and it was my job to hold the dog.

Well, this day, it wasn't much of a hunt. Just about everybody we knew had that edge on hungry then, took a gun and bullets to get squirrels, and there really wasn't much of anything left in the woods to hunt with a dog.

When our dog finally got on the trail of something that day, it was a raccoon, and it ran up a tree. My dad and granddad looked at that tree, looked at supper sitting up there in it, and went to chopping on it.

See, you hoped the chopping spooked your critter, and he tried to go somewhere else, and you could let the dog loose on him, but when he didn't do that, well, you get invested in the chopping, and you'd just go ahead and do it.

So they did.

And I was holding the dog. Turning the dog loose right is harder than it sounds. You don't want him caught by a falling tree, but if you don't let him go soon enough, the raccoon will get away and get up another tree.

Well, that's exactly what happened.

The tree fell, I let the dog go too late, and there we were looking at supper up another tree.

My daddy whipped me to within an inch of my life. Granddaddy finally told him, "That's enough, save your strength, we still got work to do."

And they started chopping on the second tree. I let the dog loose right that time. And we ate meat for supper. There was a pack of us, it wasn't much meat, but it was, you know, strength to work another day.

Migrant Work Stories

Belle Glade, Florida

CAN'T TO CAN'T

A WOMAN: I came from Georgia. My daddy and mama came from Georgia. When I was a child comin' up, I cut cordwood, you know what that is? Picked cotton, chopped cotton, hoed cotton, kept babies. Didn't have much chance to go to school, my mama and daddy had children to help with the work, not to send them off to some school. Since I come to the muck in nineteen and fifty-five, I started picking beans. I went up the road picking beans. I've been in camps that was a cot to sleep on with thirty other people in the same room, a sort of a roof over your head and not even screens on the windows. Picking is hard. It ain't easy now, but it is not as hard as it used to be, and the pay is better now. I also picked oranges, cherries, celery, tomatoes, parsley and escarole lettuce, and a bunch of those things takes crawlin' on your knees to pick, and what don't take crawlin' takes being up in the air. I chopped cane, too. You know, before I got old, I used to ask people about sixty or seventy, "How do a person be when they get old," and every single one of them told me they didn't know, I'd have to find somebody older than them to ask. But now, I got old and I found out myself. And my old days is best. Better than younger. I'm not crawlin' across fields no more in the cold or the heat, one is as bad as the other. I used to work from "can't to can't," that was from before daylight to after dark, and sometimes, they'd shine lights for us to work beyond the can't. I worked right up to "don't," and I don't work like that no more. I cook some for people now, I don't mind that, and I help people with folks that's really got old, and I don't mind that, I get on my bicycle and go where I want to go. My old days really is the best so far.

BEANS

A WOMAN: I've followed the season for beans, used to be mostly beans here, now it's corn. And yeah, the work is hard—mostly, it is just long and boring—but the pay is not as bad as it used to be, and the camps aren't either. I'm not telling you they are the Holiday Inn, but they are not as bad as they used to be. I've had fun in the camps. Used to build a fire outside at night, smoky fire to keep the bugs away, and sittin' around singin' and tellin' stories and swappin' lies. That was fun. And you were all in it together. Everybody pulling his own weight, you had to, to stay on a crew, so you were with people you could depend on. I liked that part. I didn't like it so much after I got married and started having children. Migrant camps are no place for children, I don't want my children to have to pick beans, I wanted them to learn to read and write. Picking is work with your back, which is fine as long as your back holds out, but you don't rebuild a back like you rebuild an engine. Can't be done, and there are mighty few things you can pick without using your back. Your own nose is about the only thing I can think of.

Jo Carson

School

A WOMAN: My parents followed the crops, and I learned early on I wasn't the outdoor type. The muck eats me alive, and if the muck is not enough, every bloodsucking bug within ten miles gets a scent of me and comes running. Flying. When I started first grade, I thought I'd found heaven. There were screens on the windows. I took to school. I begged to be left here when my parents would leave to follow the season, I begged to be left with anybody, and there were years when I'm the one who found people who would take me in, and I'd do housework for my board so I could be in school for the whole year. I knew from the minute I stepped through the door of a school the first time, that it was my ticket to a different kind of life from the one my parents lived. I don't know where children come by such knowledge, but some do, and I was one of them.

Peppers

A YOUNG MAN: I wanted to earn some money one summer during high school, and I signed up to pick peppers, some friends and I. They put us in the same group with these four older women, and we looked at that and thought they've dumped these poor workers on young, strong men. Right. Well, we started faster than the women did, the women didn't start slowly exactly, they just started at a pace they could maintain. And a hundred bushel baskets of peppers later we were way out in front of them; two hundred, we weren't as far out in front; three hundred, the women are even with us; and four hundred, they are so far past us, we can hardly see the dust they were raising. And they were still working at the same speed they started that morning. They were the strength out there, not us. They were the knowledge, we certainly didn't have it. It is another world, picking. They taught us to pick peppers. Next day, we didn't try to get out in front of them, we just tried all day to keep up. Tried for the rest of the season to keep up with those four old women. They were amazing. Thing I remember best from that summer was how easy the first hundred baskets a day were to pick, and how hard it was when you get to about five hundred. Those women spent the day talking, laughing, picking peppers. We spent it picking, didn't find much to laugh about, and didn't have the energy for much talk.

Summer Day

Port Gibson, Mississippi

With Money

A YOUNG WOMAN: Lots of teenagers in my day had cars or had access to them, and it was very easy to run to Vicksburg. There was always some place to go. There were lots of trips to swimming holes around: Rock Falls, Widows Creek. Summers were just kind of long and lazy. Got to where I could read three books a day as long as they were *Nancy Drew Mysteries*. The way our family was set up, you had to be at breakfast every morning, and you had to come downstairs dressed with your face washed and your hair combed. After breakfast, you figured out what you were going to have for lunch and you went to town. This was a shopping trip, often for the makings for lunch or supplies for projects. From about ten till noon, everybody worked on a project, something practical. This was handwork, and every girl was expected to know how to do it. We made quilts or did tatting. Then you had lunch and you listened to the radio, you got recipes from the radio, and you had to be very quiet while that was going on, and you kept on being quiet till about three o'clock. If you weren't asleep, you were expected to read. If you had inclinations towards poetry or art, this was the time for that. At about three o'clock, everybody would get up and take a bath. You always had to look nice. That was a real part of Port Gibson. We were taught that in deference to others, to show respect for others, you dressed nicely, you didn't go running downtown in shorts. Was not done. At four o'clock, if nobody was at your house—there were days for this, Tuesday was our day to receive—but if nobody was at your house, you'd start on rounds, you'd call on your neighbors, and you'd have a glass of iced tea or lemonade or a Coke. At five o'clock, my grandfather went for a walk and I often went with him. It was a very orderly life, you didn't have to wonder what was going to happen next. Now, we had a lot of help, but every picture I have of my family is of someone working with somebody else. Dinner at six o'clock. When I was walking with Grandfather, we often passed Oak Square, and at that time, the whole block was grown-up, it was a tangled mess, you could hardly know there was a house there. And once, he said, "Some day, our house will be like that. You'll grow up and get married and go off with your husband and there won't be anybody around to take care of anything." I had an awful picture of our house grown-up in vines and said I wouldn't let it happen. He said, "You live your life and don't worry about the house." Well, I have, but that house is not grown-up in tangles. My husband and I live in it, I brought him here. I don't do much handwork in the mornings now, other things occupy my time, but dinner is at six o'clock.

WITHOUT MONEY

A YOUNG WOMAN: The day starts before daylight, the time doesn't matter much to anybody except Daddy when school is not in. Daddy got to be at work at seven-thirty and he's usually got a couple of things he needs to do around here first, and Mama's feeding the baby so he's not crying, and I fix Daddy some breakfast and pack his lunch. Then Mama and I eat. Then everybody else is up and eats. I have five brothers. Mama said she kept trying for another girl but I'm the only one they got. I wish there was another girl. Mama and I could use an extra pair of hands. The boys have jobs they got to do, everybody has jobs around here. Mama and I clean up breakfast. Now, there is the regular work has to be done, the washing and ironing and mending and cleaning and cooking, and the baby, but summer's got the garden, too, and Mama and I will put up at least five hundred quarts of food before the growing season is over. If it is not at least five hundred, Mama worries about what we're going to eat for the winter. I told Mama I'm gonna marry a man rich enough to let me buy my food at the grocery store. She said that is a fine idea but I still better know how to grow it, said nobody plans on being poor. So from the time of the last frost, we are working in a garden, and we grow it from the seed we saved from the year before. By the time school is out, we are already putting food in quart jars. Lots of early stuff in the garden, like lettuce, is just for eating; it don't can, but early stuff like peas you do can. We grow every kind of bean you can think of, and tomatoes and corn, peppers, cabbage and okra. Squash. Potatoes. Onions. You name it. We make kraut, we make pickles. If it grows in the ground and it can be eaten, Mama and I grow it and we preserve it. The boys are sent after berries or whatever fruit is in season, and we can that, too. Or dry it. Pick what is ripe the evening before or at first daylight, break the beans, skin the tomatoes, cut the corn off the cob, peel and cut up everything, cook it, and put it in jars. We even can meat when the animals are slaughtered. If we're picking cotton somewhere else for wages, all this food work needs to be done before the dew is off the cotton in the morning, 'cause once the cotton is dry, you start picking it. But make this day easy, say we are not picking cotton. Mama and I do laundry for eight, including a baby in diapers. We've got running water, but we don't have a wash machine, so we heat the water in pots in the yard and do our washing there. We do another family's washing, but there are just four of them. Mama and I make some extra money. We're going to buy a wash machine when we got enough. We dry the laundry on a clothesline and we iron it. And in the meantime, we've fixed a noon meal for seven and cleaned up, and started dinner for eight. And we've also done all the work in the garden. The minute something is give out, Mama plants something else, she doesn't waste the space, and we do that. She don't trust the boys to do it. They do the hoeing and the weeding. Daddy plows, but it is us that keeps the plants in the ground and the produce coming. Mama said to me when she died, her ghost is likely to be back here trying to can tomatoes. Mama says the way to get out of this is to get educated. She tells me this almost every day we are standing over the stove sealing mason jars. I can't tell you how much I like school. I'm thinking maybe I'll study physics or the stars or something. It is the furthest thing I can think of from string beans.

Wal-Mart

East Tennessee

INTERVIEWER: How did you come to have a clothing store?

SHOP OWNER: My father.

INTERVIEWER: And it just suited you? All puns intended . . .

SHOP OWNER: No, I hadn't planned on it, but when I got home from that war . . .

INTERVIEWER: World War II? You're not old enough for World War II . . .

SHOP OWNER: And not Vietnam either, too old for that. Korea. Nobody thinks of Korea. I commanded a platoon, nineteen months and three days, and nobody ever thinks of Korea. The most profound experience of my life, and it is forgotten. Nobody ever thinks of Korea.

(The Interviewer exits.)

But I got home, I had fifteen hundred dollars to invest, and my father and I bought a clothing store. He kept a salesman's job to help pay for it, he liked the travel and meeting people. But what I wanted to do was to just be still somewhere safe, and a clothing store seemed pretty safe, so it worked out. It was fun. People had a good time dressing themselves up in new clothes. Going shopping was a bigger event then than it is now, new clothes were for something, and a woman might go to the hairdresser before she came here, because she wanted to know how she was going to look in what she bought. She'd bring her husband—I can't really recommend shopping with husbands—or her mother or some friend, and it was an event, and it was fun to watch. Fun to be part of. New clothes made a person feel good. Men, too, men just weren't as much fun, I guess it was because new clothes were harder to come by then than they are now. People were closer with their money or they didn't have so much of it. People shop for recreation now, something to do, go out and spend money, and buying new clothes is not the same kind of event anymore.

That's what Wal-Mart has done.

When Wal-Mart came in here, my business fell by three quarters and I lived with that for a while, and then I shut the store down and went on a tour of Wal-Marts. I drove all over the South looking at Wal-Marts, walking around in them, I drove from Wal-Mart to Wal-Mart, not town to town, and I'd park in another huge parking lot and walk into the store and walk the aisles. At first, all I could think of was, How can I compete with this? I can't. And for a hundred Wal-Marts, that was all I could see: I can't compete with this.

And I started home, I was going to close the store, go out of business, find something else to do.

And as I was driving home, I started thinking, It is so big, it's got to have cracks in it.

And after all that traveling, I came back here and went to Wal-Mart one more time. I knew my way around a Wal-Mart pretty well by then, they are all laid out the same, but this time I am looking for what they didn't have. It is an odd way to look at a store like that. And it is the last thing they want you to do, they want you to see what they've got, that is why it is all out on shelves like it is. Grocery stores do the same thing, you buy more if you see it all. But what I had to do was find the cracks, and I could sell what they didn't.

What I knew was clothes. So I went through the clothes racks at Wal-Mart, looking at the brands, looking at seams to see how their merchandise was put together. And it wasn't hard to imagine a little up market, I could carry a better line of clothes, and I could advertise my clothes that way, and I did it: "Buy clothes that don't fall apart in the washing machine." And the next year, my business was back up a little again, and by the next year, I could afford to stay in business. I turned myself into a marketing man, marketing to the cracks in Wal-Mart.

It won't last, somebody with more money and a plan will figure out how to market to the same Wal-Mart cracks, and they'll come in with a chain store and a huge parking lot, bound to happen, but this will get me through to retirement.

I was the interviewer who forgot Korea. For experiencing that moment, it won't happen again. I kept the moment in what I wrote for two reasons. Maybe somebody reading this won't forget Korea, should the need arise to remember it. The second reason is harder to explain: I found the experiences he related parallel, the forgotten war and the forgotten legion of shopkeepers at risk in the face of ever-expanding Wal-Marts or whatever else might be ever-expanding. One is hot with bullets; the other has no bullets, but I suspect it is almost as pressing if you are the man touring Wal-Marts looking for the cracks to try to market to. What happened for me after I heard this story was that I began considering how I spent my (decidedly modest amounts of) money. I had heard the arguments before I heard this story, this isn't a new problem at all, but I'd never listened to a man who was so affected by the economic tidal waves that are embodied in the likes of Wal-Mart, before I listened to this one.

I once studied geography, this is an idea from economic geography: it used to be said that money could be expected to turn over at least seven times in a community before it left that community. This simply isn't true anymore, seven times is too many turnovers to expect locally in a global economy. But because of this story, I now play an ongoing game with myself. I try to spend most of my money in those places that are the most likely to spend the most of that money again locally. I'm not likely to ever get seven local turnovers for a dollar, that time is past, but if I'm careful, I might actually get three or four. This is a slightly different way to think. If you like it, feel free to use it.

Children

Lonely

East Tennessee

A WOMAN: I was raised lonely, my parents both died when I was little, died of the smallpox, and the aunt who took me in never wanted any children, so she never had any of her own.

I was not a child in that house, I was a sort of live-in-servant from the time I got to be about eight or nine.

Before that, I was supposed to be . . . well, it was like I was a piece of her furniture. She covered her furniture with sheets so it wouldn't get dirty except when company came, and maybe once a year she had some company, and then she took the sheets off the mail-order furniture. And me, she dressed me like I was a doll, also from the mail order, and I spent a lot of my time sitting very still, being quiet. She didn't like noise any better than she liked dirt. I always halfway expected her to put a sheet over me.

I ran away with the boy who was to be my husband, William called Bill, when I was fourteen years old. I knew how to cook, how to wash clothes and raise food, it was me that did all that in my aunt's house by then, and why shouldn't I do it for myself instead of for her?

My husband and I got married by jumping over a broom together. For our twenty-fifth wedding anniversary, we got married in a church.

I told him the first night we spent together that I wanted children, that I wanted so many children I couldn't count them, I wanted as many children as we could feed even if all they were eating was beans and cornbread, because I didn't want to ever be lonely again, and I didn't want my children to be lonely, and I didn't want him to be lonely if something happened to me.

And we had children. Seventeen living. I bore the first when I was fifteen. Rebecca, Rachael and Ruth were my first three. And then my first set of twins, Michael and William. And then another set of twins, except one of them died, James, and Joshua was living. And then three more girls, Ellen, Constance and Bernice. And then four boys, Ben and Lawrence and Carl and Fred. And then I lost one that I always just called Angel. And then four more girls, Elizabeth and Barbara and Harriet and Cecile. Cecile was born when I was forty-two. And we fed them everyone, and sometimes it was just beans and cornbread, but nobody was hungry and nobody was lonely. They might have wanted a little for privacy, but they had somebody to talk to, and they could always go out of the house if they wanted to be alone. I only ever had the doctor out here twice. Once was when Ruth got an abscess in her leg and he had to lance it, and after that, I knew how to do it. The other time was when Lawrence broke his arm and the bone punched through the skin. I set the other broken bones, and bound them up till they healed. We didn't have that many. When they had the mumps or the measles, I put all of them that had it in the same bed, and doctored them myself. We lost a son, Michael, to the war; a daughter, Ruth, in a car wreck; and Elizabeth got bit by a snake when she was ten and died. The rest are alive and married now, except Rebecca, the oldest, who says she helped me raise one family, she don't want a second one, and she went to college on her own and works at a bank now. She paid the two youngest through college.

Some of my children has and wants more children than others, but four seems to be the limit. Not a one of the living remembers their childhood as lonely, and they are not lonely now, and Bill and I are not lonely old people stuck off somewhere by ourselves, and I tell them all to thank the aunt who showed me what lonely was.

No

East Tennessee

A WOMAN: Now, I had twelve children, but it was because my husband, never in his life, understood the meaning of no. He went to his grave, me a yelling, "No!" in his ear, and he went anyway.

Shared Younguns

East Tennessee

A BLACK WOMAN: I don't know if the whites did it, but we would share younguns. Lots of black families did. If somebody died, we'd send a child to stay at that house as long as they were needed. I went to live with my grandmother when Grandpa died. I mean, I went to live there, not just visit for a week or two. And then, there were the ones that never could be mothers. I was one of those, and my sister sent one of her sons to live with me. I raised a nephew, and then he moved back in and lived with me again after my husband died.

Lives with me now, him and his wife. He's as much my son as anybody's.

One Child

East Tennessee

A WOMAN: I never had but one child, and I was a little long in
the tooth to be having a first child—I was past forty. I knew
the danger of it, but you don't risk anything, you don't get
anything either, and I had wanted a baby for years and not
had one.

Well, when I got pregnant, I went to this young specialty doctor because I was older and I knew I was more
likely to have problems, and he kept telling me I had to be
careful, that I ought to stay in bed after six months, that
I shouldn't do anything hardly, that I ought to come into
the hospital and lay there on my back for the last month of
the pregnancy, all sorts of stuff like that. That it would
probably have to be a cesarean, because my body wouldn't be
able to handle a natural labor, I mean he had me scared, and
a little mad, too. Forty is not dead yet, and I was not then,
and never had been, some sort of hothouse flower.

So I went to my old doctor for a second opinion, and he
told me not to worry so much, that worrying would mess me
up quicker than anything, and do whatever I felt like doing.

So I was stocking shelves at the store when my labor
pains started, and went home, and went to bed, and told my

husband to get the old doctor, not to bother with the young one. I had my baby in the same bed I was born in, my old doctor and my husband delivered her, and she was as fine and fit and fancy as a newborn baby gets. She is a joy to this day.

Only Child

East Tennessee

A WOMAN: I was an only child and it was my daddy's doing. I was a hard birth, I was breech, and my mother had been in labor a long time and was about to die of it, and the doctor hauled my father into the bedroom, and said you have to hold a leg, and got her sister to hold the other leg, and took a hammer and chisel out of his black bag and broke her pelvic bone right then and there. He got me out of her with us both alive, bound her up, and said to lay there and not move for six weeks while her bones grew back together.

Well, she was fine, she healed fine, and she wanted more children, but my daddy said he was never doing that to any woman again, especially not to one he loved.

I have no idea what they did with, for, or about sex, that wasn't something either of them could have talked about, especially not to me, but they stayed with one another, and I was the first and only child of their marriage.

Missed Children

Etowah, Tennessee

A BLACK WOMAN: The housework black women did was hardly ever just housework, it was usually minding the children of the household, too.

And my mother did "housework," did it because she had to have the money to feed us (my father died in an accident at work when he was thirty-two), but she spent more time with those children than she did with her own.

Now, we had a real community in Parkstown, my brothers and I checked in with a neighbor when we got home from school, we had people we could go to if we had a problem. They knew Mother and knew her situation, and we were not neglected.

But from the time I was eight years old, I was responsible for my younger brothers. I'd get them to school because Mother had to leave early (for a long time, she had to walk to her job). I'd get them home from school, I'd get our supper, because Mother often didn't get home in time to do that.

I guess it didn't hurt me. Well, I know it didn't, but I missed a lot of childhood and I really missed my mother.

She was raising somebody else's children for the money to feed her own, and hers weren't very welcome in that other household. When she was there, it was like she wasn't supposed to have any other life.

None of the people she worked for—three families over thirty years—kept up with her after she was too old to work anymore, and only one of them—one of the children she helped raise—came to her funeral.

All this made me mad for a long time, mad enough to march on Washington and Selma, Alabama, and a few other places under the leadership of Dr. King.

Now, with children of my own, it makes me really sad. For her. I missed part of a childhood, but I got a fire lit in me in exchange for it.

My mother missed her children.

Sixteen Children

Harlan, Kentucky

A MAN: Mine is such a story of this place. My mother and daddy married when she was fourteen and he was nineteen, and she started having children. Daddy took over his father's farm and mined coal. We had it better than most because we lived in our own house and we used the land for a garden and animals.

There were sixteen of us children. I was number twelve.

Daddy built some extra rooms on that house but there were still two or three or four of us, depending on how big we were, to a bed.

Mother cooked and washed clothes and preserved food and raised children.

She went to church on Wednesday night and Sunday morning, so we did, too. I don't remember hearing her say anything much. I'm sure she did, but I don't remember it. I do remember her pointing to one of us and then to a job to be done.

We all worked. Daddy worked a job in the mines. My sisters helped Mother; my brothers and I did a lot of the farmwork: plowing, planting, harvesting. We grew a lot of corn, most of it for food for the animals. There were stories about people having to help a cow to her feet so she could start grazing in the spring, after bleeding her during the winter to make blood gravy for starving people, and it was a point of honor with Daddy that we weren't ever going to do that. So we grew lots of corn.

Vegetables, we must have had three-quarters of an acre in shelly beans.

And the animals. We kept hogs for meat, we'd slaughter two or three at a time depending on how big they were. The cows were for milk, but we kept and ate the steers. A mess of chickens.

And a couple of mules to plow and pull a wagon.

We had a car, too, an old Model A Ford was the first I remember. You had to back it over hills because there was no fuel pump in it, it was a gravity-feed fuel line, so the gas tank had to be uphill from the engine. Wasn't much use around here. Daddy drove Mama to church in it, but it was mostly for show. Wouldn't even hold all of us. So going to church, there'd be Mama and Daddy in the car and the rest of us straggled out behind, walking.

As we got old enough, we all hunted, the girls, too. Mother insisted the girls learn to do that. We ate everything. Deer, bear, snakes, possum, porcupine, fish, squirrels, birds. With eighteen to feed, everything was meat. About the only thing we didn't eat was vermin and pets and mules. We kept a team of mules.

Daddy worked with his mules and he loved them. Every one I remember that we had were just really good animals, and they were more of a source of pride to him than that car.

That was Mother's car, except she never drove it.

It was hard after my father died, he was killed in a mine accident, but we had the farm and the house. Mother didn't want us boys in the mines, but the farm wasn't enough. There were still five children at home when I left home at fourteen. I went North. Pittsburg. Worked in the steel mills. Sent some money back home for a long time. About as hard as coal, I think, and almost as dangerous.

Then, I saw a chance to change my fortune, and I joined the army. Spent two miserable years almost getting killed daily in Korea, and came home and went to school on the GI Bill. I graduated from college when I was thirty years old, which is old to just be graduating, but I was working through that, too, and I never regretted the time it took.

I taught English and social studies.

The day I was packing my bag to leave home, my mother found her voice . . .

"When you marry, you marry a woman who can say no to you and make it stick. Sixteen children is fourteen too many. We've done all right, we've not starved and you've had shoes on your feet when you needed them most, and your daddy and I loved every one of you, but this way of life isn't available anymore, and this world won't support everybody having sixteen children. You need to do something different."

I married just such a woman. We have three children, one more than my mother thought was enough, but we had choices my mother and father never had. You know, I think of all us children packed four to a bed, head to toe, like sardines, and part of me remembers it with great love, and part of me wonders how in dickens we all lived through it.

Healing

The Cures

A combination of places

The cures have been collected from everywhere I've worked thus far. One of the standard questions asked of everyone who gives stories for any of these projects is if they remember any traditional folk cures or medicines their parents or grandparents used. The pickings from a generation (or a place) that did not have easy access to doctors or modern medicine are almost always rich. This has consistently been women's knowledge; this stuff came down through generations along with cornbread recipes, the secrets of good potato salad, and the obligation to mop the kitchen floor once a week. More, they have been astonishingly consistent from place to place. Sometimes ingredients differ by what is available in a given place and I've played some with the differences for this piece, but the differences are never big.

I've used these cures, or some of them, three times, different ways, in different plays. For this collection, I've organized them like a call-and-response, a litany in church. Except I don't want them exactly like a litany, I want them more bound to the earth and human, so I've added lines (comments, spoken by multiple women)—things people really said about one or another of the cures—like commentary.

COMMENT *(A woman)*: From the old collection of women's knowledge:

CALL: For the sting of a bee

RESPONSE: put chewed tobacco on the sting.

CALL: For the vomiting

RESPONSE: chew the root of the blackberry brier.

CALL: For the thrush

RESPONSE: find a woman who's never seen her natural father . . . She must pull with her hand a leaf from a pear tree, put it in her mouth and get it wet, and put it in the baby's mouth. Cures the thrush in babies or grown people.

COMMENT: She don't need a pear leaf, all she has to do is breathe three times for three days straight into the baby's mouth. But she has to be a woman who has never seen her natural father, and then some of them can't do it.

COMMENT: Some I know cured thrush by rubbing the baby with their hands.

COMMENT: I've heard of that, but I've not seen it done.

CALL: For sore throat

RESPONSE: gargle salt.

CALL: For a cough

RESPONSE: lemon, honey and whiskey in hot water.

COMMENT: Skip the lemon, honey and hot water.

CALL: For indigestion

RESPONSE: asphidity dissolved in moonshine.

CALL: For an ailing in the stomach that asphidity don't fix

RESPONSE: chew pine buds.

CALL: For cleaning out the body

RESPONSE: a dose of castor oil.

COMMENT: You can use the store-bought stuff like castor oil if you don't have the gumption to collect ginseng, but ginseng tea made with the root will clean and tone and make you feel new again.

CALL: For a burn on the skin

RESPONSE: pee on it.

COMMENT: Some can talk the fire out of a burn.

CALL: For the poison ivy

RESPONSE: juice of the jewelweed.

COMMENT: You know, don't you, to look next to the poison for its cure. Jewelweed grows close with poison ivy.

CALL: For a soreness of the body

RESPONSE: camphor dissolved in moonshine and rubbed into the muscles.

CALL: For a puncture with a nail

RESPONSE: put the nail in a pot of water, add turpentine in, and boil, and hold the wound over the steam.

COMMENT: I'm telling you, pour straight turpentine on the wound. It hurts pretty bad, and you jump around for a while and make the wound bleed clean, and you don't get the lockjaw.

CALL: The boils

RESPONSE: a salve of cactus root and other wild and growing things.

COMMENT: Cactus root, where am I going to find cactus root?

CALL: For cleaning out the body

RESPONSE: a dose of Epsom salts.

CALL: For female troubles

RESPONSE: the root of blue cohosh.

CALL: For pain of the extremities

RESPONSE: a hot soak in Epsom salts.

CALL: For the fevers

RESPONSE: a tea of fever grass.

COMMENT: Fever grass? I never heard of fever grass. It's fever weed, also called snakeroot.

COMMENT: It's fever twitch.

COMMENT: Fever twig

COMMENT: also called bittersweet.

COMMENT: Or feverwort, which is boneset.

COMMENT: It's feverfew, it's just plain old chrysanthemums, you use the leaves and flowers, and it is also good for colic in babies.

CALL: For worms

RESPONSE: the bark of dogwood.

COMMENT: I use the seeds of Queen Anne's lace.

CALL: For excess water in the body

RESPONSE: horse-balm tea.

CALL: For a sprain

RESPONSE: a poultice of the boiled leaves of the peach or pear tree.

CALL: For a cold

RESPONSE: a bib made of beef fat and tied onto the chest.

COMMENT: No, that's got to be onions or ramps fried in beef fat, and made into a poultice and laid warm onto the chest.

CALL: For the whooping cough

RESPONSE: a hog-toe tea.

CALL: For the mumps

RESPONSE: corn-shuck tea.

CALL: For the measles

RESPONSE: a tea of sheep pills.

COMMENT: You know what sheep pills are? Sheep crap, and the specific instructions are to wrap a little wad of it in a piece of clean cloth, like using clean cloth makes any difference, and boil it, and drink the water. Just boil it a long time. Won't do any harm.

CALL: For pneumonia

RESPONSE: a tar jacket.

COMMENT: That didn't work for me, but the warm poultice of onions and ramps is good, same as for a cold.

CALL: For anemia

RESPONSE: the juice of collard greens and beets.

CALL: For earache

RESPONSE: human pee, baby pee is good.

COMMENT: You'll not put pee in my ear. I always used peach seed crushed in a clean rag, wet and warmed in boiling water and dripped into the ear, but I got the peach seeds from my husband's people down in South Carolina.

CALL: To stop bleeding

RESPONSE: Ezekiel 16:6.

COMMENT: We always used spiderwebs, we never had much luck with Ezekiel.

CALL: To bring milk down in humans or animals

RESPONSE: massage by hands that have smothered a mole.

CALL: A sty in the eye

RESPONSE: rub the eye with dew-wet moss.

CALL: For infection in a wound

RESPONSE: maggots.

CALL: To regulate menstrual periods

RESPONSE: worm-worked turpentine balls rolled in flour. Three pills a day, skip a day, three pills next day, skip a day.

CALL: For leg cramps

RESPONSE: place the shoes under the bed as if they were taking a step.

CALL: For a hard labor

RESPONSE: a knife under the bed to cut the pain.

CALL: For the kidneys

RESPONSE: yellow root.

CALL: For the liver

RESPONSE: yellow root.

CALL: For the stomach

RESPONSE: gopher-grass tea.

CALL: To clean the blood

RESPONSE: sassafras root as a tea.

CALL: For warts

RESPONSE: stump water.

COMMENT: That's an old wives' tale. Common milkweed is good for warts, you use the sap.

CALL: For boils

RESPONSE: a poultice of jimsonweed.

COMMENT: Just don't let anybody eat any of it. It'll poison people. Don't let horses or cows eat it either. Makes them crazy.

CALL: For the seven-year itch

RESPONSE: a wash in turpentine and sulfur.

COMMENT: Shave the hair of the body, smear the body in turpentine and sulfur, boil the clothes and bedclothes in lye soap. Do this every day for two weeks or you'll get reinfested with lice. That's why it's called the seven-year itch.

CALL: For arthritis

RESPONSE: *(No response)*

COMMENT: I know what the plant looks like growing in the woods, but I'm so crippled-up with the problem, I can't go look for the cure.

CALL: For depression

RESPONSE: hard work.

CALL: If a man has caught a fire

RESPONSE: *(No response)*

COMMENT: Is it holy fire? That won't burn him.

CALL: If a man has caught just regular a fire

RESPONSE: roll him in a rug. Throw dirt on him. Do pee on the burns.

CALL: If a man has stepped into a nest of bees

RESPONSE: run for water and get in it.

CALL: For the good of a child's character

RESPONSE: a whipping a week whether they need it or not.

CALL: For the good of the soul

RESPONSE: a verse or two every day until the Bible is by memory, if you live that long.

I've left out most of the cures I know to be truly bad medicine, like putting butter on a burn, but I've kept some I suspect are equally as bad simply because they are so odd, like sheep pills for measles. Measles is a virus and nothing we have works on viruses. On the other hand, I have no notion of what you've got chemically when you've boiled sheep pills; maybe some pharmaceutical company should check it out.

I recommend a tetanus shot in preference to turpentine for a nail-puncture wound, but this cure comes from a time before an easy trip to a doctor was available, and I suspect the turpentine business is better than nothing.

But then, there are things here like the thrush cure . . . I met a woman who qualified (never met her natural father) who was asked regularly for her services to cure thrush in babies and she evidently did it with considerable success. She was introduced to me as "the best cure for the thrush I know" by the local doctor who sometimes sent her patients. Thrush (Candida) can be very hard to get rid of. What she did was breathe into an afflicted baby's mouth, or so she said.

I suspect milk might be helped to "come down" by massaging the breasts in women who are nursing or need to be able to nurse (brand-new baby), never mind the smothered mole, but if a person really believes "hands that have smothered a mole" help, they probably do. Pity the mole. How do you catch a live mole anyway? The baby could starve while you are out catching the mole.

Peeing on a burn is actually a good idea, the mild uric acid is good for a burn, and pee is the closest thing you have to sterile liquid readily available in your body. Your mouth, your spit, is anything but sterile. So, how about the story of the man whose motorcycle, then his clothes, caught fire, and he was standing on a street in Boulder, Colorado, stripping his burning clothes off when a man walked up, hauled out the necessary equipment, and peed on him. "Hold still, son, this will keep the burns from being so bad." I'm not just making that up.

I have no idea about baby pee or peach seed for an earache, but the peach-seed cure shows up with astonishing regularity.

I don't hold much with knives under the bed as a cure for anything. Sounds like a way to plan a murder . . . "Well, Officer, the knife was under the bed to cut cramps, see, and I had this nightmare, and before I knew it I'd stabbed him sixteen times . . . It was an accident." I am making that up.

And last, I think the whipping a week is a truly terrible idea. I included it because I've seen it so very often.

Healer

Colquitt, Georgia

This is from a play in which I used some of the folk cures. The Questioner is a folklorist collecting the cures. He has asked earlier in the play about faith healing and has been directed to find a specific woman.

A Woman with a satchel comes on stage. She is followed by a Child and the Questioner.

PART ONE

CHILD: That's the woman you're supposed to talk to. Mother says she's nice and funny.

QUESTIONER: Now that we've found her, what am I supposed to say to her?

CHILD: Ask her if she's the healer, I guess.

QUESTIONER *(To Woman)*: Are you a faith healer?

WOMAN: Lord, no.

QUESTIONER: Do you do faith healing?

WOMAN: I am a minister of faith.

QUESTIONER: Do you cure people who are sick?

WOMAN: I don't cure anything. Curing and healing are very different, not the same at all. Curing is science, healing is something else. Part emotion.

QUESTIONER: What is in your satchel? Kleenex for the ones who cry?

WOMAN: Just stories. At the moment. But the satchel is also good as a carry-on bag. Fits under the seat or in the overhead compartment, either one.

QUESTIONER: Heavy load for a bunch of paper.

WOMAN: There is no paper, the stories are not written down.

QUESTIONER: What are the stories about?

WOMAN: How to live and how to die.

QUESTIONER: Why would you carry around stories about how to die?

WOMAN: Everybody is going to do it, every living thing on this Earth dies, and part of healing is accepting that. When I was a child, I had fallen and cut my knee. My mother said to wash it and go back out in the sun and play, and that would cure it, but I could not quit crying. And she said, "What? Do you think you are going to die of a cut knee? You will die after it, seventy or eighty years after it, if you are lucky, but you won't die of this cut knee." I think of that.

QUESTIONER: You are the last person I'm gonna call if I get sick.

WOMAN: Good idea. Call the doctor first. Take your medicine as prescribed. But listen . . . you don't want to live forever. How boring that would be. Think about it: "There's no reason to get up this morning, I'm never going to die. Might as well just stay in bed." So you spend the next hundred years in bed. And you roll over and yawn and you have all the time in the world, so you take another nap. It is the temporal nature of this life that makes it so delicious. Think about that when you roll over in bed again and stretch and yawn on Saturday morning.

PART TWO

QUESTIONER: So what is healing?

WOMAN: An opening, an act of faith of the person who is healed.

QUESTIONER: Faith in God?

woman: Belief in God is one way to express faith.

questioner: Are there others?

woman: Oh yes.

questioner: You're not fixing to hug a tree or something, are you?

woman: Not anytime soon. But now that you mention it, there are a couple I'm very fond of in my front yard.

questioner: Oh, wonderful.

woman: Listen, Thomas . . .

questioner: My name isn't Thomas.

woman: Listen, Thomas. If a person's faith is such that hugging a tree is an expression of their faith, then hugging a tree is an act of faith. Do you follow that?

questioner: I guess.

woman: Try again, Thomas. The whole business of faith is for connection to a power greater than your own. It does not matter at all what name you give the power. A faith that is common among us, like Christian faith in Christ and the Bible, gives us a way to talk to one another about the power of faith. And you know "Thomas," so when I call you that name, it means something, because we have the story of doubting Thomas in common, and that is very useful. But healing by faith is very old, very, very old, older than Christianity, so evidently it does not matter what name you give the Power, or how you try to tap into it. You do whatever works, and what's very funny is that whatever you believe can work, does work. So, yes, hug a tree if it works for you.

Part Three

questioner: What do you do to heal people?

woman: Of what? Warts? I send them out for stump water.

questioner: Say, cancer . . .

woman: I told you, I don't heal anybody. A person must open themselves to healing. It is not that they must heal themselves, that would be a terrible responsibility, wouldn't it?

"Go! Sit in a corner till you're well or till you're dead!" Healing is not that. A person must learn to open themselves to possibility of being whole, that's what healing is, and sometimes that means letting go of a tremendous amount of worldly baggage. And you wonder what I carry around in my satchel.

QUESTIONER: What should a person do if they have, say, cancer?

WOMAN: Laugh. Laugh long and hard. Sing songs, make a joyful noise. Go fishing. Or golfing. Or riding a horse, whatever makes you feel one with your body and soul. Pray and mean it. Accept that nobody lives forever. What do you want? A list of things to do to put in your notebook? A tea of fever grass? Do what the doctors say if that is what feels right. Trust what you know in your heart and act on it. Take risks. Breathe deep. Go to sleep to learn from your dreams. Wake for the joy in the day. Let what is past go. Touch people who care for you. Let them touch you. Touch the creatures you care for. By all means, hug a tree if you want to. Lay down on the ground in the sun and try being the part you are of this astonishing Earth. Watch out for the fire ants. Now, you want the list for high blood pressure?

QUESTIONER: I guess. Sure.

WOMAN: It is the same.

QUESTIONER: This is pagan, witchy, touchy-feely, new-age blasphemy.

WOMAN: Watch out, or I'll squint one eye and chant the Twenty-third Psalm at you.

QUESTIONER: What do you call what you're doing?

WOMAN: I don't try to name it. I'm just telling you that your body has its own knowledge, a knowledge of the universe, because it is of the stuff of the universe and not separate from it, do you hear that? Your wonderful rational mind says I, I, I. "I think, therefore I am." I think, therefore I can collect cures; I think, therefore I can learn how to solve problems. And so you can, but you can also think yourself into isolated, miserable corners, and you can worry yourself very sick with that same wonderful mind. Your body knows other older connections with things beyond your rational knowledge. Healing is finding, relearning if the truth is spoken, those older connections. And faith in a power greater than your own is part of it. So find some way to believe in God.

QUESTIONER: And your part? What is your part?

WOMAN: I help with the worldly baggage. That's all.

Voodoo

―――――――――――

Chicago, Illinois

A Man and three women: the Man's Mother, the Mother's Sister Bissa and the Voodoo Woman. All are on stage in different places from the beginning of the story. Use the stage as a tour of the events in the story. The Man is the one who moves. He must travel with his Mother to get to Bissa, travel with Bissa to get to the Voodoo Woman; then, he must pass Bissa and his Mother again on his way back out with new understanding. It is a formal version of the classic hero's journey.

MAN: I was not an easy kid. I was a liar and a thief and I didn't do my homework and didn't like school and I hung out with a bad group. I was a half-assed juvenile delinquent. But my mother was no charmer either. She was a controlling woman, and her punishments were sometimes close to torture. She'd of been in trouble with the Geneva Convention folks and I've got the scars to prove it. She was a professing Christian, and she spent a lot of time at church, so for a long time I spent a lot of time at church, but it didn't make any less a sinner out of either of us, it just made us feel guilty about what we did do, which made us even meaner to one another. My mother came from the South, Deep South, backwoods people, and she'd worked hard to get to Chicago, and then to make something of herself when she got here. And she had made something of herself, she was a nurse, and from all reports, a good one. I never knew her as a nurse. If I was sick, I got locked in my room with a pot to shit in, a pitcher of water and some crackers, while she went and did her eight-hour shift. I'm not making that up. This was junior high, somewhere about seventh grade, and I was sick for almost a month. It was right after that I started getting into real trouble, and she sent me to the voodoo woman.

(A car made of two chairs. The Man's Mother is in the driver's seat.)

MOTHER: Get in here.

(He enters his Mother's sphere.)

MAN: She picked me up after school in a car. We didn't have a car, and I didn't even know she knew how to drive, but she did. And she drove me out to O'Hare Airport, drove like a bat out of hell, and it turned out she had an airplane ticket, and she was trying to make the connection. The ticket was for me. *(To his Mother)* Where am I going?

MOTHER: You'll find out. Bissa's gonna pick you up when you get there.

MAN *(To the audience)*: Bissa. Her big sister. Bissa was short for "Big Sister." I was scared sometimes of my mother, but Bissa struck terror in my heart. I mean Bissa could pick you up by the scruff of the neck and sling you like a cat against the wall. And Bissa didn't mind doing it. I mean, I had been partway through one wall already, the wall between the kitchen and the bathroom in our house, thanks to Bissa, when she came to Chicago for Thanksgiving, and I hadn't really done anything that bad. I'd talked back to mother in her presence. And then we had to get through Thanksgiving dinner, my collarbone was cracked, and my manners

weren't all Bissa thought they ought to be. She had my
mother in tears all through dinner and I was afraid to eat
anything. May have been the only time in my life I was ever
afraid to eat. I mean, I've been in jail, and I've been in some
tight situations, but I've not since been so scared to sit at a
table and eat. Bissa. But at least I knew where I was going.
Back South. Bissa still lived back where Mother started. *(To
his Mother)* Do I have to stay with Bissa?

MOTHER: While you're there, you get to.

MAN *(To the audience)*: "Get to," you hear that, "get to" . . . *(To
his Mother)* How long am I going to be there? *(To the audience)* But she didn't answer that. She popped me on that airplane—no luggage—just barely in time to take off. It's my
only airplane trip so far.

(He leaves his Mother and passes to Bissa's sphere.)

Well, Bissa met me at the other end. Bissa was not as big as
she had been. Truth was, Bissa was dying. This was the last
thing she knew to do for her sister, try to help her with me.
Truth was, Bissa had bought me the airplane ticket. But
I didn't know all this then. Bissa put me in her car and we
drove through the town where she lived. We drove for a
long time, out into swamp country. I've never seen anything like it. *(To Bissa)* Where are we going?

BISSA: You know when we get there.

MAN *(To the audience)*: We must have driven forty, fifty miles,
and we come onto cars parked by the side of the road out
in the middle of nowhere, and Bissa pulls up behind the last
one and parks.

BISSA: You got an appointment, all these others just waiting in
line.

MAN *(To Bissa)*: "In line" for what?

BISSA: To see the Sister. She's gonna put some starch in you,
straighten you right up.

MAN *(To the audience)*: And we walked down a path that led into
the woods, and we came to a clearing and a little one-room

cinder-block building that didn't seem to have any windows. There were people seated around outside on benches, maybe eight or nine men and women, and there was a woman beside the door to the house. Bissa told her who we were and that we had an appointment, and she told us to take a seat. We sat. No one spoke. We all just looked at one another. A man came out of the house, and then the woman by the door called my name . . .

(He leaves Bissa's sphere and enters the Voodoo Woman's.)

. . . and motioned me into the little house. There was no light inside the house except what came in the door, and, as I had thought, no windows. It didn't smell dirty, anything like that, but it was damp, you know, concrete damp. A tiny woman lay on a little bed and watched me come in. At first I didn't see her, my eyes weren't adjusted to the dark.

(Voodoo Woman, VDW, looks at him for an uncomfortably long time.)

VDW: So you're the bad boy, are you? I don't see nothing so bad about you. What do you do that's so bad?

MAN *(To VDW)*: I don't like school.

VDW: I asked you what you do that's bad. I didn't ask what you thought about school. You lie, son?

MAN: Sometimes.

VDW: Um-hum. You take things?

MAN: Only if . . .

VDW: Do you take things don't belong to you?

MAN: Sometimes.

VDW: Sometimes ain't no answer. Have you taken things that don't belong to you?

MAN: Yes.

VDW: Ma'am!

MAN: Yes, ma'am.

VDW: Um-hum. You a liar and a thief. You ever murdered anybody?

MAN: No. *(He remembers)* Ma'am.

VDW: You ever cut up on dogs or cats or other living things just
for the fun of it?

MAN: No . . . I wouldn't.

VDW: You ever set fire to things or pee your bed?

MAN: NO! Ma'am.

VDW: So you're the kind of boy does little bad things.

MAN: I guess so.

VDW: You guess so?

MAN: Yes, ma'am, I do. But, Mama, well, Mama . . .

VDW: You fixing to tell me your mama whips on you?

MAN: Yes . . .

VDW: Sounds like she should, boy, you a liar and a thief.

MAN: She gets madder than that.

VDW: Oh.

MAN: It's like she stays mad and it doesn't matter what . . .

VDW: Oh. So you're telling me your mama whips and whips and
whips on you, and it don't do no good anymore 'cause she
already whipped on you for everything she can think of.
And, now, you just waiting to get old enough to leave
home.

(No response.)

Am I right?

MAN: They don't try to find you after you're sixteen. I mean
you're supposed to be eighteen, but nobody looks for you
if you're sixteen already. Not in Chicago. I don't know
about here. And I'm fourteen almost and—

VDW: Here. *(Hands him a plastic baggie of something)* This be a
kind of memory powder. Every morning, you take a pinch
and you put it on your tongue, and as it melts, you remember that easy days go faster than hard ones, and if you don't
do something to make her mad, the days will go faster for
you. Now, go and take your powder and think about get-

ting through high school before you're so anxious to leave home. Go.

(He enters Bissa's sphere again.)

BISSA: What she say to you? She tell you to behave like you're supposed to? What she say?
MAN *(To Bissa)*: She gave me this.
BISSA: What is this?
MAN: It is powder to make me do the right thing.
BISSA: Aw, hell, she supposed to put a spell on you, just her powder don't work no better than what you get at the drugstore.

(He leaves Bissa's sphere.)

MAN *(To the audience)*: I wondered, for years, how that old woman could have looked at me and seen so much. Bissa drove me right straight back to the airport, she didn't even feed me supper. I got on another plane and got into Chicago about midnight. Mother was there to meet me.

(He enters his Mother's sphere again.)

MOTHER: You learn anything this afternoon?
MAN *(To his Mother)*: Yeah.
MOTHER: What she tell you?
MAN: To behave.
MOTHER: She put a spell on you?
MAN: I think so.
MOTHER: You feel any different?
MAN: I think so.
MOTHER: Let me see the powders.
MAN: How do you know about the powders.
MOTHER: Bissa called and told me. *(She tastes them)* This is just baking soda. Hell. All that money for a damn bag of baking soda.

(He leaves his Mother's sphere and is by himself.)

MAN *(To the audience)*: It did taste like baking soda. Memory powder evidently does. I took those powders a pinch at a time, the bag lasted about six months, and the old woman was right, the easy days did go faster. After that, my memory was better, I didn't need the powder anymore. I won't claim I was any better in school for my visit to the voodoo lady or that I quit lying or that I quit taking things sometimes. I didn't. I did quit throwing things so much in my mother's face, I tried harder to stay out of her way, and it did make what was left of our life together easier. I left home at sixteen.

This was a journey that was even more mythic than it looked as I wrote it, but you saw some of that if you saw it on stage. The oral history itself was not nearly so coherent as it seems in the story I wrote. It was about forty pages of difficult stuff, and the first difficulty was that it was difficult to read at all. My job was to glean something useful. An abusive mother was there, fearsome Bissa was there, and the trip to a voodoo woman kept coming up as maybe the most important thing that had ever happened to him. I basically ignored everything else but these things. This man had pulled his act together sufficiently to move from homeless to a single-room occupancy hotel, an SRO, in Chicago. The play was made of stories from people who lived in the new SRO; all of them had recently been homeless. This man played himself on stage. What he said of this piece was that he hadn't understood how important this story was to him until I wrote it like I did. I think about that. I'm writing this paragraph more than ten years after I wrote that play, and I still think about his remark. All of us have these mythic constructs in our experience. You can make a version of the hero's journey out of almost anybody's life; we are a hero unto ourselves if to nobody else. Almost everybody has some version of Sisyphus's endless labor, too, and if we're smart, we've already done Camus's turn on it for ourselves. Do I not sit at this computer seemingly endless hours? And when something is done, do I not start back at the bottom again with something else? And haven't I come to love the work? Well, yes. I think many of us never find or understand how these old myths might apply to our lives, and seeing such an application is sometimes a terrific revelation. I do love this stuff, and, sometimes, writing these stories, I get to play with it.

Part of this man's deal for getting into the SRO was that he would get a GED and a job. I hope he did it. He's already faced the voodoo woman, the GED (with some study) should be a piece of cake.

Midwife

Walton County, Florida

A NURSE: There is one story I want to tell. I was there, I was assisting Mother, so I was witness. This girl came in, she was young, she said sixteen, but I had my doubts. I'd say thirteen or fourteen. She came in with her mother and her boyfriend. They brought her. She was white, she was poor, she was filthy, like she had been rolling around in dirt, she was undernourished, and she was having a baby. A child having a child. She had had no prenatal care, hadn't been to anybody not even once, hadn't been to the doctor herself since she was a baby, and she had been in labor almost thirty hours already. They came in a storm. They banged on the windows to be let in. The girl was exhausted and crazy with pain and afraid she was going to die. We had to hold her down to keep her from falling off the bed to try to get the baby out of her. She'd run out of the energy to jump off things. It looked like she had already been doing that. She was the very kind of patient we didn't want—a high-risk delivery—she should have been in a hospital. But her mother and this boyfriend didn't take her there. And the storm was bad, the ambulance couldn't get out here to us. Didn't know when they'd be able to get here. The baby started to come, except it wasn't a head, it was a foot, and then, at least, there was a second foot. We held the girl down, tried to get her to breathe and push. My mother and I both looked at those little feet and they were chalk white. There is only one thing that means, the baby is dead. We had to grab those little feet and help. It wasn't coming out on its own and the girl wasn't helping. And it was chalk white all over, it had the umbilical cord wrapped around its neck, and it was a girl and it was as dead as I've ever seen a new baby. My mother turned her upside down and back up, put her in warm water, blew air into her lungs, did everything she knew to do. Nothing. The girl's mother said, "It's dead," before we did. And then said, "You poisoned her with that brown stuff." Make me so angry . . . They'd done nothing for this girl or her baby, and we had done everything we knew to do. We had given her blackberry tea. We give every woman who comes to us blackberry tea. It settles the stomach. I turned away because I couldn't look at the woman or that girl, and I heard my mother say, "Dear God, if you want me here, I need a miracle now." I looked at her and she turned away from the baby, too. We both knew what this would do. This was the ammunition Florida needed to put her out of business. We all just stood there, not long, but it seemed like a very long time. And a voice said, "Look again." I heard it, and my mother heard it, too. And we both turned to look at that dead baby, and we stood there and watched her turn pink and start to cry.

This story wants a little explaining, the midwife of the title's name was Gladys Milton, a black woman who was recruited and trained by the state of Florida, and sent into the upper reaches of a poor county as a midwife. She delivered more than three thousand babies successfully over many years (she judged potential high-risk pregnancies very well, and sent them to a hospital). But the state of Florida decided they no longer wanted her in that business; she wasn't a registered nurse. She fought the decision in court and won. This story happened as her case was coming up in court. Gladys Milton died in the mid-nineties. It is her daughter, an RN who still runs the same clinic, who told this story.

Great-Grandmother

East Tennessee

CHILD: Tell me about the grandma.
WOMAN: Aren't you doing homework?
CHILD: It helps me.
WOMAN: Hearing about your great-grandma helps you do your homework? Right. How many times you heard this?
CHILD: She was an Indian.
WOMAN: She was a Cherokee woman.
CHILD: And she had a husband.
WOMAN: She said he was "too pretty to work."
CHILD: He sat on the front porch.
WOMAN: Best I know she was married to him. But, yes, he sat on her front porch, days on end, summer, winter, and the only thing I ever knew he did was serve as bed warmer.
CHILD: What's that?
WOMAN: That's for me to know and you to wonder . . .
CHILD: She was a doctor.
WOMAN: She was a midwife and an herbalist. She helped women who were having babies . . .
CHILD: She helped the babies get born.
WOMAN: That's it.

CHILD: And she went out in the woods and got plants and made medicines out of them. If I had an earache . . .

WOMAN: Peach seed.

CHILD: She'd have put a peach seed in my ear?

WOMAN: She'd have made you a medicine with a peach seed. You know the truth? I was a little scared of her.

CHILD: You never told me this part.

WOMAN: Oh, yes I have. I just never said it quite that way.

CHILD: She was mean?

WOMAN: She was hard. She was fair, but she was hard, and you had a lot of work to do when you went to visit her.

CHILD: Like hoeing in the garden and milking cows.

WOMAN: Right. And washing dishes and washing clothes . . .

CHILD: I know about jobs. I carry out the trash. Why were you scared of her?

WOMAN: Imagine if your grandma came in carrying animals she'd killed, and you knew you were going to eat them for supper.

CHILD: Grandma buys chickens. You buy chickens.

WOMAN: Yeah, but they are ready to cook and they come from the grocery store. Imagine squirrels and rabbits. Imagine your grandma carrying in a whole deer. Imagine a bear.

CHILD: You ate a bear?

WOMAN: I ate part of one. When you were at her house, you ate what she cooked whether you liked it or not.

CHILD: She cooked a bear?

WOMAN: She hunted it, and killed it, and skinned it, and tanned its hide, and cooked the meat. She used the bearskin as a rug on her floor during the winter.

CHILD: People would come up to her house.

WOMAN: People would come up to her house when a member of their family was sick and tell her what was wrong with them—sometimes she'd go off and visit the sick person— but most of the time, she'd go into her root cellar.

CHILD: It was like a cave.

WOMAN: Sort of like a cave. It was dug into the ground and the earth made a roof over it, so it was dark and cool. A lot of it was lined with stones. Had spiders in it. She had a big root cellar, almost as big as your bedroom, and she kept her medicine herbs there. She kept food in there, too, in the front part. She might send me after potatoes or apples or onions. But if she was making a medicine, she'd light a lantern and go in there and shut the door, and she'd be gone for a long time sometimes. You could hear her, sometimes she sang a song . . .

CHILD: Like a Sunday-school song?

WOMAN: It wasn't a Sunday-school song. I think it was a medicine song.

CHILD: Do you know it?

WOMAN: I wish I did. She didn't let anybody else in there with her when she was working on medicine. Ever. And she'd come back out, sometimes with a salve, or sometimes with a mix of leaves and roots that you made tea out of, and that would be the medicine. Lots of people came to her for medicine and she'd give them what they needed.

CHILD: And they didn't pay in money.

WOMAN: Nobody had much money then, but they might bring food or something like that. They might bring a hen that laid eggs. Or a ham. Maybe some cloth.

CHILD: And she fixed 'em 'cause she knew about the woods.

WOMAN: She fixed a lot of them. There are some things even the woods won't fix.

CHILD: And you're kin to her and I am kin to you.

WOMAN: You're kin to her, too. She was my grandmother and your great-grandmother.

CHILD: Do you think she would have liked me?

WOMAN: She would think you are too soft, that your life is much too easy. She thought my life was too easy. But she liked me, and I bet she'd love you.

CHILD: I wish I could know stuff like she knew.

WOMAN: Me, too. I just remember a little bit. I do remember going with her up on the mountain to collect plants, ginseng and jimsonweed and burdock. And laying the leaves and roots and flowers all separate out on flat rocks to dry.

But I never saw her mix them up. She didn't let anybody watch. She died when I was just a little older than you are now.

CHILD: She didn't know how to write.

WOMAN: I don't think she knew how to read or write, there was never anything to read in her house, not even a Bible. I never saw her do either of those things, so all that stuff she knew about the plants . . .

CHILD: She died.

WOMAN: And all she knew went with her.

CHILD: That's the bad part.

WOMAN: Yes, it is.

CHILD: Some day I might write down things I know. 'Specially if I get to know a lot.

WOMAN: That, my little question queen, is why it is important to do your homework, so you can get to know a lot.

CHILD: But I'm never going to know what she knew, am I?

WOMAN: Not the way she knew it, no. I don't think there is any way anybody could know the way she knew, not anymore . . .

Fiddler Slave

A YOUNG BLACK WOMAN: My great-grandfather was a fiddler. He was born and died a slave. What little I know is that the people who owned him hired him out: he played white folks parties, dances, weddings from Natchez to Vicksburg for many years.

He lived to be an old man. He was kept mostly in the house, not sent to the fields, because no one wanted to ruin his fingers for making music. He was evidently a fine fiddler.

The only other story I know of him is that he once rode one of his owner's race horses, a horse he wasn't supposed to ride, but a horse he thought he could ride that nobody else could, brought it back with the dawn, and was not whipped for it.

I never met him, he was dead long before I was born. I barely knew my grandfather, he was an old man when I was born. But it may be true that the inclination to music is inherited. Someone gave my grandfather and my father and me music . . .

I know how odd this is to say, but if we do come back into this world in some way, I want to invite my great-grandfather to come back now, as a son or daughter of mine. I promise the best raising I can give, and I also promise, if the calling is still there, a fiddle as soon as hands are big enough to hold it. I promise teachers if they are wanted, and I promise a mother whose heart flies on fiddle music.

I do not promise to make it easy, I cannot, this world is not so predictable as that. But I can promise life would be different—he would not be born to bondage this time. Things that come too easy have no value anyway, and charms for an easy life don't work, not in my experience.

But music . . . music is a salve for the soul, and maybe you have to have been in need of a salve to know what a grace salve is. But I think you can learn that in any life.

So, my ancestor, come back if you want to. Just know you are invited. Wanted. Needed. There is never enough of good fiddle music.

Things to Say

Harlan, Kentucky

A MAN: We went over to that museum, the Coal Miners Museum; you had to drag me, but you know me, that sort of thing isn't my cup of tea. Not my can of beer. So you drug me anyway. And I was sort of a stick in the mud for some of it. I mean, I've been down the hole, I've seen the coal face plenty more than once. Why do I want to go to a museum about what I do for work?

But there was something there I've been thinking about. Those letters. Notes. The last words of a man who knows he is dying to the people he loves back up top. Lord help me. You got a cave-in or something, you are running out of air, or you are hurt and you are running out of the will or the ability to live, and you know it. And you search your pockets for anything, a grocery-store receipt, anything. And then maybe all you've got to write with is your own blood, so you say, "I love you," in blood, because "I love you" is what is most important, and that's what you've got room for on the Sav-A-Dollar piece of receipt paper. Well, I've been thinking about that. And I've got more to say than that, so I want to try to say some of it here and now.

Elizabeth, my wife, you have been the making and the breaking and the breaking and the making of me. Time and again. What else is a marriage? And I love you beyond what I can say. Part of that is because I'm not real big on saying things, part of that is because some things are almost too big to try to say, and part of that is because this language isn't big enough to really say love.

My sons, James and Paul, my daughter, Melinda, I see myself in all three of you, my little assortment of graces and my failings. You are the wheel of time as it turns for me. You are my life ongoing along with your own. Can a man love something better than his own life? Yes, he can. I just don't think he can say much about that either.

This place, this house, those things I do, my habits, my can of beer, the Corvette I've spent a small fortune trying to make run right, I love them, too. Not the same way, but they are the little investments of my days, and if I would love myself, I have to love them. So let me say this too: I love this life that is my life.

There will be a time when I leave this life, there is not one of us gets out of this world alive, and I pray my leaving is not some morning at the coal face by some mistake or lack of adequate safety 'cause somebody's trying to save another dollar, or some other act of God. I would like to die an old man in a comfortable bed. I'm gonna be afraid, I think everybody's gonna be at least a little bit afraid when that time comes, but I don't want fear and regret to be the only things I'm feeling.

That is why I decided to try to say some of this now.

I have loved and been loved beyond anything I can name or understand, and I have been amazed. Just know that I have been and I am *amazed.*

Faith

The Carmen Miranda Hats

Colquitt, Georgia

A WOMAN: I had an aunt who never missed a Sunday of church in her life. She lived to be an old lady, she married and buried eight husbands. I guess she buried them during the week so it didn't interfere with Sunday service. The last one she got from a MALE-order catalog, or so it is told.

She was a big woman, he was a tiny man, but they evidently loved each other because they always held hands, and during that time, she was given to lots of white face powder and Carmen Miranda hats.

Now, Carmen Miranda was a Latin singer whose trademark was skimpy Caribbean-looking outfits and hats, huge hats with wide brims, piled with fake pineapples and cherries, all sorts of fruit and vegetables, eggplants, tomatoes, yellow squash, whatever could be used for color. And stuffed birds. And miniature buildings. And ribbons, and sequins, and those little dangly ball things that people sometimes use for curtain borders hung around the edge.

These were extravagant, amazing creations that started something of a fashion rage, and, in Carmen Miranda's pictures on her record covers, they didn't seem quite so out of place as they did on Sunday morning, in Colquitt, in church, on my aunt.

She sat right down front. She was big enough that if she kept her head tilted right, the little husband could also sit under the hat. And she sort of created her own amen corner because she was a shouter, and she'd get into it.

And she'd fan herself in the heat, and white powder would blow off. Looked like some sort of spaceship, that hat with the powder blowing out from underneath it, onto the husband, onto the people in the pew behind her. You could go home from four pews back and brush white face powder off your clothes.

After the eighth husband died, she gave up the Carmen Miranda hats; it may have been him that loved them on her, and she was a little more conservative with the face powder, too, and she never married again. She didn't live that long herself.

But she was in church every Sunday she was alive, and she kept up her part of the amen corner.

Baptism

Belle Glade, Florida

An assortment of children, six or seven of them, play this scene. They range in age from about four to twelve. Bea is the oldest at twelve. The Girl Cousin is just a little younger than Bea and very prissy. Bea and the Girl Cousin's lines are assigned. Give the other children the other Cousin lines as they are capable of handling them.

BEA *(To the audience)*: I had this cousin.

A COUSIN: A *girl* cousin.

BEA: I had lots of cousins.

A COUSIN: Boy and girl.

BEA: But there was one cousin that kept me in trouble. Everything I did, she told my mother when Mother came in from picking.

GIRL COUSIN: "She ate all the peanut butter and wouldn't give us any."

BEA: Whether it was true or not. *(To the Girl Cousin and her mother)* "Mother! The jar was already empty, I just licked it!"

GIRL COUSIN: "She chased Huey with a snake."

BEA: "I chased Huey with a stick, I said it might be a snake 'cause he was chasing Bitsy with a baby alligator!"

GIRL COUSIN: "She bit my dog."

BEA: "'Cause he was chasing the chickens! And I tried to stop him and he was going to bite me and . . ."

GIRL COUSIN: "He's got a bloody ear."

BEA *(To the audience)*: I bit the dog. He quit chasing chickens.

GIRL COUSIN: She shouldn't have made a hole in his ear.

BEA: I got paid back. He tasted awful.

GIRL COUSIN: She hurt my dog.

BEA: I was the oldest child of us and all our parents went to the fields to pick, usually beans, they all specialized in picking beans and I was supposed to be in charge. The others were supposed to do what I said. In the morning the grownups would say, "Now Bea is in charge, and you have to do what she says." But it didn't work. It only worked that way till they were out of sight. Easier to herd cats. And this one cousin . . . I hated her. She was so prissy, and she wouldn't clean up after herself when I had to make us lunch, and she was a snitch.

A COUSIN: A fink.

A COUSIN: A rat-fink snitch.

BEA: Now, about that time, I got saved. Our church held the baptizing down at Twenty Mile Bend, at the bridge, they'd take you into the water, there'd be the pastor and two men helping him, and the water there was up to their waists, so it was up to the middle of my chest. And you'd wade in with the men that were helping you, and the preacher would say, "I baptize you in the name of the Father, of the Son, and the Holy Ghost, and then he'd dunk you over backwards, and you were supposed to come out of the water a better person with your sins washed clean. And I felt like a better person, or I think I did. Except the more time I spent with this girl cousin, the more I thought about being able to wash some of the sin out of her. So, one day it rained for most of the day and the ditch in front of the house was full of water. Full. Waist deep on us, and we'd been playing in it since it quit raining, and the sun came out and got hot again. All except this cousin, and she didn't want to get her clothes wet.

GIRL COUSIN: Don't touch me! I'll tell my mama if you do . . .

BEA: I think we're gonna hold a baptizing.

BOY COUSIN: I'll be the preacher!

A COUSIN: I'll be the preacher, I'm bigger than you are.

BEA: I'm gonna be the preacher.

BOY COUSIN: You're a girl.

BEA: I'm the oldest, so I'm the preacher!

A COUSIN: Do me!

A COUSIN: Me first!

BEA *(To the Girl Cousin)*: I think we have to baptize you.

GIRL COUSIN: I'm not ready, and it is not a real baptizing, and I don't have to play.

BEA: You are ready, and it is real too.

GIRL COUSIN: I'll tell!

BEA: This is religion, you got to do it, and I'm telling you to get in the ditch! Get her in the ditch.

(The Girl Cousin is put in the ditch by the other Cousins.)

GIRL COUSIN: NO!

BEA: Hold her down! This is serious!

(Bea, with help, forces the Girl Cousin over backward.)

I baptize you in the name of the Father . . .

GIRL COUSIN: Let me loose! I'm gonna tell, and my mother is going to whip you and your mother is . . .

BEA *(Dunking her, holding her under; the Girl Cousin fights)*: I baptize you in the name of the Father and Deuteronomy and Ezra and Isaiah and Daniel in the Lions Den and Job and Meshach and Shadrach and Abednego and Moses and all the animals that went on the ark, like cats and ostriches and crows and snakes and cows and chickens and dogs . . .

(She has run out of things to name, but she is still holding the Girl Cousin underwater.)

A COUSIN: You're gonna drown her . . .

BEA: I'm not, I'm just making sure she's cleaned out of all her sins . . . and bears and . . . what's another animal?

A COUSIN: Elephants?

BEA: Elephants and giraffes and lions and tigers and panthers and peacocks and ducks and turkeys and . . .

GIRL COUSIN *(Gets a gulp of air)*: HELP!

BEA *(Putting the Girl Cousin back underwater)*: And Pastor Williams and Mother and Daddy and Aunt Jane and Uncle Tommy and Buster the cat and trees and grass and flowers and eggs and peanut butter and jelly sandwiches and recess and . . .

A COUSIN: Mules?

BEA: Mules. And the Father, and the Son, and the Holy Ghost. Amen.

(The Girl Cousin is finally allowed up.)

Go and be cleansed of your sins, like telling on everybody all the time.

GIRL COUSIN: I'm gonna tell!

BEA: You tell, and that means the baptizing didn't take, and we'll have to do it again. Maybe do it lots more times, and I'll have to think of all the animals instead of just some of them.

(The Girl Cousin considers this information.)

Some people have to get saved seven or eight times before it really takes.

GIRL COUSIN: How come you think you know so much?

BEA: 'Cause I've been baptized by the preacher. And I'm older than you. And I'm smarter, too.

A COUSIN: And she's meaner.

BEA: Now, go over there, sit down, and dry off. And don't tell anybody ever.

A COUSIN: Yeah. Don't tell.

A COUSIN: Or she'll do it again.

BEA *(To the Girl Cousin)*: Or I'll do it again.

(The Girl Cousin sits by herself, with all the others watching, and makes some effort to regain her dignity without falling to tears. To the audience:)

So my tattletale cousin sat down, dried off, and bit a hole in her tongue when the adults got home, but she only need one. When her mother asked what had happened to her clothes . . .

GIRL COUSIN: I fell in the ditch. By mistake.

BEA: So it was a successful baptism. Very successful. Just took that once.

The Call to Preach

Newport News, Virginia

A MAN: I was an unlikely candidate for a call to preach. I could not say three words running without being silenced by my own mortification, but my father was a preacher, and maybe the work is in the blood.

I had come home from church one Sunday mad enough to sling a bull by its tail and about the right age to try. We'd heard what seemed to me to be the same sermon for the forty-ninth time, preached by my father, directed at me (in my opinion), the one on pride.

When my father came home, he said if the sermon bothered me, I needed to listen to it, but to be careful, some day I might find out how hard it was, especially when the congregation didn't see something you knew you were seeing.

How it stayed on your mind and you had to keep talking about it.

That is very true. I talk so much about the necessity for community now, I know there are folks who go home wondering if I don't have another sermon I could dig up from somewhere and dust off.

My father asked me shortly after that Sunday morning if I ever thought of preaching, and what I said surprised me: some day I felt I might have a call, and if I did, I would try.

And about that time, I had a dream: I was by myself in a room with four books laid out on a table and I was to choose one of the books, and the rest of my life would depend on which one I chose, and in the dream it became very evident that the one I am to pick is the second book from the left. There is nothing on that book to separate it from the others. I don't even know what the books were, but the one I was to pick was very clear, and in the dream, I knew it.

Well, I was twenty-two when the call came, just married, and my name had come up with some others for a second preacher in the church, and the congregation had the option of choosing among us themselves, or to ordain by lot.

When my father saw it was me going to be one of the choices—preachers were chosen from the congregation— he called the bishops in to run the election. He didn't want anyone thinking he was trying to influence a vote.

And the congregation decided to choose by lot.

Choosing by lot is a way to let the Lord choose; it is also a way so there are no hard feelings, no politics at all. And the Sunday of the choosing, the bishops interviewed four of us in the afternoon and found us all worthy, and that evening in church, there were four books—hymnals, it turned out—each with a piece of paper folded into them, and one of those pieces of paper said yes. The books were lined up on a table and we were each to choose one.

And the moment I saw those four books, I knew which one was mine. The second book from the left, and I knew, even before the bishops opened it, that it was the one with the paper folded in it that said I was to try. And so it was. That was how I knew I was supposed to preach, that I was called to it.

I was a very odd preacher at first, tongue-tied and without enough experience to come anywhere close to wisdom, and no opinions on anything except cows I dared venture. I took my texts straight from the Bible. And the sermons were very short.

Some may wish I was still so tongue-tied, I don't know. They are generous enough not to say so if it is true.

I know my father sat in the congregation and pitied me—at first, I pitied him having to listen to me—but every other Sunday was my turn, and I did it.

The Postman

Colquitt, Georgia

A MAN: I was twenty-two, twenty-three, somewhere in there, and I went to church because it was my raising.

If you didn't go, the folks at the church would come out to your house, ask you what was wrong with you. Why weren't you in attendance? What was more important than the worship of God on Sunday morning? I would have liked to have had the opportunity to say, "Lying in the bed," or something like it, because I would have liked to have seen the face of any deacon I knew when I said it. But I would have had to have said, "I am not in church because I am a sinner and I like it."

I am not a liar. A sinner, yes; a liar, no, and I would have had to tell the truth. And I didn't want to have to say it to some deacon looking at me over the dinner table—that alone would be enough to put you off your dinner—so I went to church and I avoided the confrontation.

Mine were little sins. I never but once struck a man in anger, and he hit me back hard enough that I didn't try anything like that again. I never struck a woman. I broke a pitcher instead once, and I hit an old mule more than I should have, but I was trying to convince that animal that kicking at people was a bad idea. These are not sins like Ten Commandment sins: "Thou shalt not kill." I'm not inclined to that or thieving or messing with somebody else's woman. But I liked a game of cards on Friday night, and good sour-mash liquor, and the company of funny men and rowdy women and dancing and singing and scraping a fiddle bow over honky-tonk music.

And this was a whole slew of terrible sins in my church on Sunday morning.

There was a fellow with the band I played with, played accordion, a French Creole, Catholic, a little fellow, and he would flirt with anything in skirts, and get in trouble, and get in fights on Friday night and get beat up, and spend Saturday morning recovering, and go in on Saturday afternoon to the priest in Donalsonville and confess his sins: "Father, I have consumed whiskey and played music and lusted . . ." (or whatever), and be absolved, and do his penance, and show up in church on Sunday morning with a clear conscience and a snow white soul, and live that way till Friday night when he got drunk and chased the skirts again.

Seemed like a pretty good arrangement to me, twenty-four hours out of the week were dangerous, but any other time he could have died and gone straight to heaven.

Not me. He was raised with that belief, and I wasn't. I wasn't saved, and I didn't want to be saved, because I liked my sins too much, and I didn't intend to stop them. But I went to church, because I didn't want to have to answer for them to some stony-faced deacon.

So, one Sunday morning I am sitting in my usual place, close to the back, and next to a post that was part of the structure of the church. I liked the post, I liked to look at it, and I liked the way it had worn from the touch of hands, I liked to think about the hands, and so I sat there. The preacher was earning his pay—I wasn't really listening very close—and a voice spoke to me: "This is the day, now is the time."

I looked around to see if anybody else had heard this voice, and it didn't seem like anybody else had. I knew who it was. There wasn't any question, and there wasn't any question what it was saying either. It was the Holy Ghost telling me to give up my ways and come clean and live a different life. It kept saying: "This is the day, now is the time." And the preacher finished his sermon and began the hymn of invitation, and it pushed me up onto my feet and I was supposed to walk to the front of the congregation, take my seat on the sinner's bench, and promise to change my ways, and I did not want to do it.

So I held to the post.

This will come again, I told myself, I don't have to do it now, another year or two won't hurt, and I clung to the post and did not go. I heard that voice, my call, a long time ago, and I am not yet saved. I could walk to the front of the church this minute and say I was saved, and be accepted.

Even now, when I am gone, people will say I was a good man because I am a good man. But I am not a liar, I never have been, and I won't start now.

I have never heard the call again. I know the most unforgivable sinner who ever comes before the judgment of God is the one who heard a call and did not go.

This man haunts me. Not literally. I don't mean to say that his ghost shows up on infrared or that it follows me around and jumps at me from dark places. I don't mean that at all. I mean that I think of him often. In the story as it came to me—a woman told it about her favorite uncle—he went to his grave believing he was going to hell because he held to the post that one time and never joined the church. His niece described him as "one of the gentlest, funniest men I ever knew" and "a really good fiddler." What I take from this story is that what we say to one another matters, it can matter a holy lot, it can affect a life as much as what we do to one another. In this same vein, I have another story of a man, also a musician, a banjo player, who quit playing anything but religious music in his thirties because he was told the Lord didn't approve of that other stuff. He acquiesced. So do you figure he got to go to heaven for that? For these people, gone though they are, just tell me what happened to the version of this particular Lord that likes a joyful noise? Who forgot that in the rush to tell somebody else how to live a life?

The Last Chance

Sautee-Nacoochee, Georgia

The Last Chance Bar, a redneck bar in Purgatory (it has a long bar).
The Bartender and one customer, Jim-bo, are there.

PART ONE

JIM-BO: So gimme a beer.

BARTENDER: You know the rules, son, you don't get a real beer,
    you just get to sit here and remember beer . . .

JIM-BO: That's partly my problem, I know I had a lot of beer,
    but I don't remember very much of it.

BARTENDER: Well, sit here for a while and see what you can
    come up with. That is exactly what the redneck bar in
    Purgatory is for. Your Last Chance . . .

JIM-BO: Could I have a bottle in my hand? That might help . . .

(The Bartender gives him a Coors bottle.)

I always had Budweiser, if you don't mind, never liked this
sissy stuff . . . .

(The Bartender trades him bottles. Jim-bo looks down the neck of the empty Budweiser bottle.)

'Scuse me again, but could it have something in it?

(The Bartender pours from a plastic bottle of water.)

If you can get that stuff here, you could get beer.

BARTENDER: Purgatory's dry. Sorry. It's the Law.

JIM-BO: Hell of a place.

BARTENDER: Not quite, friend, not quite . . .

JIM-BO: Can you tell me again why I'm here?

BARTENDER: Well, there's several theories.

JIM-BO: Yeah, I know, I know about some of that . . . But nobody's praying for me, so tell me something else this time.

BARTENDER: My opinion, most likely you're here because there was unfinished business back on Earth . . . So just sit here and think about that for a while. We don't ever close, so you've got plenty of time.

(The Bartender goes about other business. Jim-bo sits, considers his bottle.)

JIM-BO: Unfinished business. That's a bad joke. All my business was unfinished business. Every single bit of it.

(The puppet of a horse, Cowboy, comes down the long bar toward Jim-bo.)

COWBOY: Where'd you go, Jim-bo?

JIM-BO: Aw, hell . . . Cowboy! You dead, too?

COWBOY: Actually, no. But this is your Purgatory, and I'm part of your unfinished business.

JIM-BO: I loved you better 'n anybody.

COWBOY: So where'd you go?

JIM-BO: Well, what you been up to, old fellow?

COWBOY: Eatin'. Hangin' out in the shade. Looking for treats. Folks got me now are good for treats. I like that. I raced for a while. Won every race I ran. I liked that, too.

JIM-BO: You would.

COWBOY: And then, well, I ran away with a few assorted riders. That was fun, and I liked it when a girl starts squealing on my back . . . "Stop, Cowboy, whoa!" Made me feel like a real cowboy. But I don't think I did myself any favors. Not really. Don't get to go much now. Nobody will get on.

JIM-BO: You're looking good. You don't look old at all.

COWBOY: The people I've got now are good to me. I'm a horse with a lot of history. Lots of folks know Cowboy stories.

JIM-BO: Know Jim-bo stories, I'd say, and you're the transportation.

COWBOY: Well, you're in some of them. They say you were a rotten drunk and I was the brains of the operation.

JIM-BO: You've not changed a lick.

COWBOY: Well, it's true. You were just the one with the opposing thumbs. Next life, I want opposing thumbs.

JIM-BO: How's your . . . *(He gestures to a hind leg)*

COWBOY: Fine, and you know it.

JIM-BO: I had you in that little cabin all winter long . . .

COWBOY: Look, I wouldn't of got so hurt if you hadn't been off drunk somewhere. Again.

JIM-BO: You got your hind leg in barbed wire. Tore a tendon. Vet said he was gonna have to put you down, said you wouldn't get over that. And I said I don't think so, for him to sew you up, and I'd take care of you. And I brought you inside for that whole winter.

COWBOY: And you spent the winter shoveling shit and trying to catch horse piss in a bucket. That was funny. I liked that part.

JIM-BO: I spent that winter changing the dressings, and getting you to walk a little so that tendon didn't go stiff on you. Keeping you warm enough to be ok when you couldn't move around very well. I kept you, Cowboy.

COWBOY: So you did.

JIM-BO: I even got them to bring you to the parking lot at the jail one time, I had that six months sentence, and I needed to smell you, put my hands on you, make sure you were ok and that you didn't forget me . . .

COWBOY: So where'd you go, Jim-bo?

JIM-BO: That just ain't a question a horse gets to ask.

COWBOY: Why not?

JIM-BO: Well, it ain't like you're a woman, or younguns I deserted, or something like that, now is it . . .

COWBOY: Did you do that, too?

JIM-BO: That ain't your business.

COWBOY: You can tell me things you can't tell anybody else.

JIM-BO: You're a horse.

COWBOY: So I am.

JIM-BO: So why should I tell you anything? Why do you think you get to ask?

COWBOY: You already said it.

JIM-BO: 'Cause I loved you better 'n anybody.

COWBOY: That's it.

JIM-BO: And loving somethin' obligates you to them?

COWBOY: So it would seem.

JIM-BO: Aw, shit, that can't be right . . .

COWBOY: Look, friend, this is your purgatory, not mine . . . I'll be back when you've had a chance to think some more. I know I'm sort of a surprise.

(Cowboy exits. Lights out on The Last Chance.)

PART TWO

The Last Chance Bar. Jim-bo is still sitting at the bar with his beer bottle. Cowboy comes down the bar a second time.

COWBOY: They've about got your room ready, Jim-bo.

JIM-BO: Where is it?

COWBOY: Well, you can answer that question yourself by answering this one: were you a bad man or a stupid one?

JIM-BO: Fine pot of beans that is! That's a damn trick question, Cowboy, that's a question like: when did you stop beating your wife? The moment you say anything, you're a wife beater . . .

COWBOY: Not quite. Think of it this way . . . The Powers That Be here don't especially like stupidity, but stupidity isn't something that gets punished. Bad is a different story. So you can answer your own question about where your room is.

JIM-BO: All I ever wanted was a little fun.

COWBOY: And you call it fun when you were so drunk you fell off my back and slept in a ditch for the night? Me, standing there with that wretched saddle still on my back . . . Opposing thumbs again. I think a lot about opposing thumbs.

JIM-BO: No, Cowboy, I don't call those times fun, ok, but I did have some decent fun getting that way . . . And you had some fun, too. You liked to go . . .

COWBOY: And the women, Jim-bo, was all that just fun, too? It could be a woman standing here asking you these questions. You'd have a whole bunch more trouble with her than you do with me . . .

JIM-BO: I was looking for love, Cowboy. I didn't find it.

COWBOY (*Falls to his knees laughing, if it can be done*): Aw, now that is a real hoot! Looking for love . . .

JIM-BO: Dammit, you're a horse, you got no right to laugh at me . . .

COWBOY: I do, oh yes I do! You think about it, you think hard, and you tell me the most fun you ever had . . .

JIM-BO: That was on your back, 'cause you liked to go, and you'd light out, and we'd fly. Run from the law . . .

COWBOY: You call that fun?

JIM-BO: It was fun, dammit. Run for the river. Run for the dickens of it. Run like nobody's business. You were a fast horse, Cowboy. I'd have bugs on my teeth from grinning so hard. You were a great horse.

COWBOY: I still am a great horse, thanks. Now, you just think for a minute about why that was so much fun.

JIM-BO: 'Cause . . . well, 'cause we were so connected. 'Cause it felt like being something other than just me when we'd go like that.

COWBOY: I thought so. And just what do you think love is?

JIM-BO: Well, what you're telling me is, it is some kind of connection.

COWBOY: I'm telling you more than that, blockhead. You can have a connection with a light socket. *(Turns to leave)*

JIM-BO: Hey . . .

COWBOY: I like green grass better. *(Turns back)*

JIM-BO: So what do you think love is?

COWBOY: Love is what makes you more than what you are alone. That's it. It is that easy.

JIM-BO: I got a different question, ok . . . How'd you know I was here?

COWBOY: Because we had a real connection. That doesn't go away.

JIM-BO: You've not suffered any for me being gone . . .

COWBOY: No. I haven't. Horses aren't big on angst. Existentialism never was my cup of tea. Don't like tea.

JIM-BO: So why are you here?

COWBOY: 'Cause somebody has to ask you the big questions, Sugar Lump. 'Cause maybe you're not smart enough to ask yourself. Why do you think you're sitting in The Last Chance Bar in Purgatory? What do you think the last chance is?

JIM-BO: I hoped it was another chance for a beer . . .

COWBOY: And the question somebody's got to ask is not just where'd you go, but why? And the thing you've got to figure out is whether a bunch of your choices were bad intentions, or just plain old vanilla stupid.

JIM-BO: Bad or stupid?

COWBOY: Not easy, not easy at all. I give you that. And I'll tell you this . . . there are people sitting in their rooms in hell right now 'cause they'd rather think of themselves as bad than stupid. Free will is a heavy trip with you humans . . .

JO CARSON

(Cowboy exits. Lights out on Jim-bo in The Last Chance.)

PART THREE

Jim-bo's at the same place. Cowboy, the puppet, comes down the bar.

COWBOY: Last chance, big boy. Third time's supposed to be the charm. You humans got some weird ideas.

JIM-BO: It's you here because you were the living thing I was most connected to.

COWBOY: That's a bingo!

JIM-BO: I loved you, Cowboy. Still do. I guess I really did love you better 'n anything. And loving you wasn't ever about changing you, making you something else, you were a horse . . .

COWBOY: So far, so good . . .

JIM-BO: I'm sorry I just left you hanging.

COWBOY: I did ok. Think, Jim-bo, think . . .

JIM-BO: I think it was pretty stupid of me not to know that stuff about . . .

(The Bartender enters.)

COWBOY: About what?

JIM-BO: About being connected to something, and how that's love and everything . . .

BARTENDER: Jim-bo, your room's ready.

JIM-BO: So this is it, huh?

BARTENDER: This way, please . . .

JIM-BO: Keep the best of me, Cowboy. What there was . . .

COWBOY: You got it.

(Jim-bo and the Bartender exit, we don't know for sure which way Jim-bo goes. The Cowboy puppet bows to the audience, and exits the bar.)